**booksonline**

Read this book online today:

With SAP PRESS BooksOnline we offer you online access to knowledge from the leading SAP experts. Whether you use it as a beneficial supplement or as an alternative to the printed book, with SAP PRESS BooksOnline you can:

- Access your book anywhere, at any time. All you need is an Internet connection.
- Perform full text searches on your book and on the entire SAP PRESS library.
- Build your own personalized SAP library.

The SAP PRESS customer advantage:

Register this book today at *www.sap-press.com* and obtain exclusive free trial access to its online version. If you like it (and we think you will), you can choose to purchase permanent, unrestricted access to the online edition at a very special price!

Here's how to get started:

1. Visit *www.sap-press.com*.
2. Click on the link for SAP PRESS BooksOnline and login (or create an account).
3. Enter your free trial license key, shown below.
4. Try out your online book with full, unrestricted access for a limited time!

Your personal free trial license key for this online book is:

8p3z-dnw4-qjt9-yxac

The SAP® Green Book

 **PRESS**

SAP PRESS is a joint initiative of SAP and Galileo Press. The know-how offered by SAP specialists combined with the expertise of the Galileo Press publishing house offers the reader expert books in the field. SAP PRESS features first-hand information and expert advice, and provides useful skills for professional decision-making.

SAP PRESS offers a variety of books on technical and business related topics for the SAP user. For further information, please visit our website: *www.sap-press.com*.

Michael Doane
The SAP Blue Book: A Concise Business Guide to the World of SAP
2012, ~ 230 pp., paperback
ISBN 978-1-59229-412-1

Sanjeet Mall, Tzanko Stefanov
Mobilizing Your Enterprise with SAP
2012, ~ 350 pp., hardcover
ISBN 978-1-59229-419-0

Chase, Omar, Rosenberg, von Rosing, Taylor
Applying Real-World BPM in an SAP Environment
2011, 698 pp., hardcover
ISBN 978-1-59229-343-8

Luc Galoppin, Siegfried Caems
Managing Organizational Change during SAP Implementations
2007, 364 pp., hardcover
ISBN 978-1-59229-104-5

Yosh Eisbart
Outsourcing SAP Operations
2009, 379 pp., hardcover
ISBN 978-1-59229-284-4

Michael Doane

The SAP® Green Book

A Business Guide for Effectively Managing
the SAP Lifecycle

Galileo Press

Bonn • Boston

Galileo Press is named after the Italian physicist, mathematician and philosopher Galileo Galilei (1564—1642). He is known as one of the founders of modern science and an advocate of our contemporary, heliocentric worldview. His words *Eppur si muove* (And yet it moves) have become legendary. The Galileo Press logo depicts Jupiter orbited by the four Galilean moons, which were discovered by Galileo in 1610.

Editor Florian Zimniak
Copyeditor Ruth Saavedra
Cover Design Graham Geary
Photo Credit iStockphoto.com/CTRd
Layout Design Graham Geary
Production Graham Geary
Typesetting SatzPro, Krefeld (Germany)
Printed and bound in the United States of America

ISBN 978-1-59229-407-7

© 2012 by Galileo Press Inc., Boston (MA)

1st edition 2012

Previous editions were published by Michael Doane under the title
The SAP Green Book: Thrive After Go-Live.

Library of Congress Cataloging-in-Publication Data
Doane, Michael.
The SAP green book : a business guide for effectively
managing the SAP lifecycle / Michael Doane. -- 1st ed.
p. cm.
ISBN 978-1-59229-407-7 -- ISBN 1-59229-407-3 1. Software
maintenance. 2. SAP ERP. 3. Computer software--Development--
Management. 4. Product life cycle. I. Title.
QA76.76.S64D63 2012
005.1'6--dc23
2012008654

FSC
www.fsc.org
MIX
Paper from
responsible sources
FSC® C014174

Contents at a Glance

Dear Reader,

Michael Doane is a veteran of the SAP business. He began his SAP career in 1995, and trust me: He saw lots of SAP products come (and some go); he saw lots of customers complete their implementation successfully (and some not); and he knows what the best (and the worst) practices in an SAP project are.

Why would someone with Michael's experience and insight give away his knowledge, almost for free? You'll find the answer in several chapters throughout this book: Being successful in as complex and life-long a venture as an SAP implementation requires some company. You'll need a network: partners, advisors, mentors. Success with SAP is about sharing. And this is what Michael does.

I'm proud to introduce Michael Doane as an SAP PRESS author!

We appreciate your business, and welcome your feedback. Your comments and suggestions are the most useful tools to help us improve our books for you, the reader. We encourage you to visit our website at *www.sap-press.com* and share your feedback about this work.

Thank you for purchasing a book from SAP PRESS!

Florian Zimniak
Publishing Director, SAP PRESS

Galileo Press
Boston, MA

florian.zimniak@galileo-press.com
www.sap-press.com

Contents

Preface

Since 1998, when *The SAP Blue Book: A Concise Business Guide to the World of SAP* first appeared, I have regularly been asked when I will put out my next book on SAP. My initial intent was to write *The SAP Green Book* in 2001. However, once I began my research into the best practices for post-SAP go-live, I realized that the vast population of firms with SAP software were still very immature in terms of their deployment. As such, proven best practices had not entirely emerged.

While the *Blue Book* was written to demystify SAP for anyone who has a stake in its success, the *Green Book* was written for firms that seek to get the most of out of their SAP investments through enlightened organizational structures and adherence to proven best practices.

In short, the *Blue Book* addresses an SAP wedding, and this book addresses the SAP marriage.

I could not write this book with confidence in 2001 or 2002 or 2003 because SAP, especially in North America, was still in a state of flux. While SAP software made great market inroads in Europe throughout the 1980s, it was still a minor player in North America until the announcement of SAP R/3 in late 1992. When I began working in the SAP field in 1995, there were very few firms that had completed successful implementations. The entirety of the industry was focused on how to rapidly and successfully implement. The predominant concern was the time and cost of implementing SAP and, unfortunately, total cost of ownership was viewed as the yardstick. This obsession with time and cost resulted in near-complete negligence regarding the best practices for post-implementation. A large percentage of clients raced to go-live...and then fell off the cliff.

Over the past several years, I have increasingly worked with firms in the post-implementation phases of SAP. When I started this research in 2001, I found that I was largely alone. The balance of thought leadership (books, white papers, Internet content) was devoted to acquiring and implementing SAP, and there was scant mention of post-implementation planning. I wrote my first white paper on the subject in 2002 and was amazed at the outpouring of emails and phone calls from far and wide asking for more. Quite suddenly, I had direct access to a number of clients who could share their experiences and, best of all, lessons learned, many of which included the unfortunate effects of rushed implementation projects. The upshot at that time was participation in a 2002 SAPPHIRE keynote on the subject of SAP Centers of Excellence.

In the years since, I have participated in formal best practices groups for large- and medium-sized firms. In addition to providing advice and performing many presentations on Centers of Excellence, I have continued to work with Michael Connor of Meridian, Brian Dahill of ASUG, the good people of CGI, and others to gather even more best practices, methods, and means for making SAP more of a driver and less of a burden for its clients.

This book is not intended to address technical or architectural SAP considerations except in passing. (There is an increasing canon for such subjects available each month.) Nor is this book intended to explore various aspects of SAP products such as SAP NetWeaver, SAP BusinessObjects, SAP BusinessObjects governance, risk, and compliance (GRC) solutions, SAP solutions for sustainability, or SAP BusinessObjects enterprise performance management (EPM) solutions. In the quest for SAP excellence and better returns on your investments, your firm may be knee-deep in any or all of these aspects; this book should provide insight into creating and maintaining an organization that will "hold it all together."

It may be that your SAP applications are in pristine condition— that SAP has run its external assessments and given you its highest marks. Excellence in SAP is to be commended. But even with excellence attained at this level, it's possible that:

▶ Business stakeholders do not have the business intelligence they need to help the business evolve and thrive.

▶ End users only fulfill the tasks they have been taught. Or, worse, they avoid using the software because they don't know how to use it.

▶ Despite a rapidly changing business climate, you have too little flexibility to do more than tweak the business processes.

▶ You collectively have no idea what effect your SAP solution has on the firm's bottom line.

If your SAP applications platform is merely a functional utility, you are doing a fine job of standing still. This book will hopefully enlighten you about how your SAP applications can be the vehicle to continuously move your firm forward.

Acknowledgments

Ever since the 1998 publication of the first version of *The SAP Blue Book*, I have had a rich network of consultants, industry analysts, SAP executives, client leaders, and journalists willing to share their experiences with me. I have attended countless SAP events, including 13 SAPPHIREs, and have taken part in dozens of webinars. Since 1996, I have provided varying versions of an SAP Executive Seminar, the foundation of which continues to be enriched by the input of many time-generous contacts. While at META Group, I had more than 400 one-hour teleconferences with clients of ERP (mostly SAP) and learned as much from my callers as they did from me.

Many people in this network have directly contributed to this book. With gratitude, I cite John Leffler and Jim Richardson of IBM's SAP practice; Mark Wilford of Accenture's SAP practice; former META Group colleagues Dane Anderson, Kip Martin, David Yockelson, Gene Alvarez, and Stan Lepeak; Donagh Herlihy of Wrigley; Michael Bovaird of Sophlogic; Brad Wolfe of itelligence; Rob Westerveldt of TechTarget; Ray Wang, Jim Shepherd, and Paul Scherer of Gartner; Pat Gray of Intelligroup; Tim Silva of Kraft; Rob Doane, David Sanders, Tom Hickerson, John Ziegler, John Bailey, Scott Lutz (from J.D. Edwards to PeopleSoft to SAP); and Michael Myers, Kay Tailor, Jack Childs, Stephen Hirsch, Shai Agassi, David Urffer, and Mike Cornely from SAP.

More recent contributors include Brian Dahill, who has been working in this space for more than 10 years; Stuart Forman, Patrice LeBrun, and Daniel Lefebvre of CGI; and Kerry Brown and Doug Shuptar of SAP. Special thanks go to Laura Zaine for incredible networking and constant friendship, as well as to Paul Kurchina who knows everyone who matters in the SAP universe.

And a final shout-out to Danielle Ouellet and Sylvie Hébert of National Bank of Canada for their contribution to "proving out" the Bridge Method for architecting and planning a Center of Excellence. Their collaboration has been invaluable.

Contact

Client and reader input is golden, and I welcome your comments and suggestions. You are invited to contact me at any time at *michael@michaeldoane.com*. Argue. Complain. Elaborate. Query. Contribute.

All contacts will remain non-disclosure.

Introduction

So your firm runs SAP business software. Congratulations?

To help you respond intelligently to that uncertain, one-word question, we offer this book. Further on, we provide a simple maturity assessment that will help you locate your organization somewhere between the poles of Thriving and Clueless.

Implementing SAP software—or any version of enterprise software—is never easy. You may have participated in an implementation yourself or simply heard "war" stories from those who did. Such stories include the business process design battles ("That's not how we've always done it!"), end-user anxieties ("I heard that after go-live we will all be fired."), budget strains ("These hidden costs are killing us."), and data migration headaches ("We have 17 codes for the same stock item.").

The change from green screen legacy applications that worked in discrete silos to fully integrated horizontal business process applications is painful. But it can also be rewarding. Down the line, of course.

SAP claims more than 100,000 clients worldwide. (Their definition of "client" is somewhat malleable; most SAP-watchers estimate the total is somewhat lower.) We have no data about how much they are getting the most out of their investment. An informal poll of a dozen analysts and consultants I know suggests a breakdown as in Table 1.

Thriving (20%)
1. Business driven
2. Center of Excellence (or equivalent)
3. Motivated, knowledgeable users

Table 1   The State of the SAP Installed Base

Crusing (20%)
1. Business involved
2. Knowledgable users
3. Some measures
Ho-Hum (40%)
1. IT led, business is distant
2. Some measures
3. Struggling users
Clueless (20%)
1. All IT, all the time
2. No measures
3. Low level of training
4. No user support

Table 1 The State of the SAP Installed Base (Cont.)

Many of us in the consulting world have stories about those 60% of SAP clients who are ho-hum or clueless about their return on investment. One of my favorites is the scion of a family-owned firm that took zero advice from his systems integrators, vastly under-spent on the implementation and training, and then wished he'd spent the money on a new winter home in Florida (where end-user training includes the positioning of lounge chairs and the mixing of Mai Tais).

There are many potential reasons why you have chosen to read this book. Here are some of the comments we have heard repeatedly over the years:

▶ "We implemented with one goal in mind: to go live. So then we were totally unprepared to run SAP."

▶ "We over-customized the software to avoid business process change. In essence, instead of getting a high-speed business railway, we configured SAP into the same business bicycle we already had."

▶ "Since go-live, our firm is miles ahead of where it was, but the business leaders keep asking us what return we got on the investment. Since we didn't measure, we can't say. We just know things are better than they were."

▶ "During the project, our business stakeholders worked with IT to make it happen. The day after go-live, they disappeared. Now IT is holding the SAP bag."

▶ "The business processes are streamlined and the reporting is rich, but no one knows how to use the software or act on the information."

Firms that adopt SAP tend to reveal to themselves "who they are." Revelations center on how well (or badly) a firm navigates the organizational and cultural changes that an SAP implementation can incite. This extends to how decisions are made and communicated, how well leadership functions on both vertical (hierarchical) and horizontal (departmental) planes, and whether vision translates into reality or into delusion.

In my many years in the world of SAP, one thing I've noticed is the fact that few individuals can ever adequately articulate why their firm is adopting or has adopted SAP. During dozens of SAP executive seminars I have provided in the past, I have asked "Why are you adopting SAP?" The response has nearly always been an uncomfortable silence followed by back and forth and sideways commentary. One such moment sums up the general experience (and I wish I had a photograph of this occasion): The client response to "Why?" was (a) the CEO looked at the CIO; (b) the CIO turned to the CFO; (c) The CFO examined his shoes while (d) everyone else looked at the CEO.

Such lack of articulation extends into implementation projects and becomes ossified in collective organizational thinking thereafter. The decision to shift from disparate and interfaced applications running on varied databases to an integrated environment is, of course, an excellent one, but such a motive does not play well across an employee population.

It may seem like a cop-out, but culture is at the heart of SAP success or failure. If your firm has strong leadership and embraces change, you will probably see benefit and enjoy a reduced level of operational problems. If your leadership is weak and your firm resists change, your SAP experience will be like an endlessly bad movie.

If your organizational culture is lacking, there is still hope. SAP can be deployed in ways that will actually improve that culture. Here is one example:

I once provided continuous advice to a CIO whose insurance firm had recently implemented SAP. The CIO kept saying that she *knew* the business processes were much, much better than before, but that business leaders, lacking perspective, felt that the SAP acquisition had been a boondoggle. Needless to say, there were no measures of "before SAP" and "after SAP," so the argument centered on subjective perceptions and not hard data.

To counteract negative perceptions and to put the firm on the path of SAP satisfaction, we sought out an ambitious business leader and asked him to illustrate a business problem that SAP might help solve. We made sure to measure actual company performance relative to the business process in question. The process was redesigned, SAP was configured to enable the improvements, and the results were measured.

This ambitious executive had the enormous satisfaction of presenting to his colleagues how he had identified and solved a business problem and thus saved the company many thousands of dollars. This led to envy, of course, but envy with a positive outcome: Other business leaders stepped forth with proposals for other business improvements that could be enabled through SAP.

Inevitably, the firm created a business improvement committee with the charter of saving the company money through the judicious deployment of SAP assets.

Result: a dramatic change in culture, keyed by (a) an understanding of how SAP can best be deployed, (b) constructive business and IT alignment, and (c) measurement. Without measurement, the business leader would have had little evidence to present to his colleagues other than what the CIO already possessed—the notion that "things are better."

The following are best practices of firms that have been successful with SAP:

► Take ownership during the implementation: Provide full-time talent to the implementation project and don't "leave it to the experts" to lead that project.

► Establish a "benefits-driven" culture and processes to exceed the base measurement of time/cost adherence.

► Extract measurable benefit from the implementation.

► Adopt SAP best practices relative to processes, rather than insisting that you know better.

► Maintain a single instance/single version (or at least a viable limit of instances).

► Take a long-term approach to SAP (beyond implementation).

► Invest in organizational change management and continuous end-user training.

► Create a Center of Excellence (or equivalent) at the outset.

► Energetically retire legacy systems (master your application portfolio).

Going live with SAP is only the end of the beginning. For many years, I have focused more time and effort on this subject than that of acquiring and implementing SAP software. In the course of my research and consulting experience, I have seen excellence at firms including Delta (my first model for a Center of Excellence), Wrigley (with a vibrant, global Center of Excellence), L'Oréal, S.C. Johnson, and Texas Instruments (where best SAP practices are born). All have wrinkles, but those will be ironed out one day.

I have also seen a major petroleum firm with nearly 300 instances on top of 300-plus JD Edwards installations; a pharmaceuticals firm with 7 separate sprawling SAP installations; another pharmaceuticals firm that spent $50 million undoing $45 million worth of ABAP customization just so it could upgrade; a wood products firm with 6 of 12 divisions on SAP and the other 6 in varying states of legacy hell; a services firm with 10% of its staff thriving on SAP and the other 90% stuck in manual labor; a small manufacturing firm with 50 users that ran through 4 project managers in less than a year; a global electronics firm that went live in more than 20 countries and then decided that it had over-customized and so started the project all over again.

While I observed positive best practices at the former firms, I have observed other practices at the latter firms that teach a valuable lesson: Don't do what they did. My concern, as evidenced in Table 1, is that there are many firms like these.

In 1995, I believed that the SAP market would be a brave new world in which IT actually served business and where technology would be seen as an enabler rather than an end state unto itself. SAP promised to free us of undue operating system concerns through its powerful middleware and, since the applications were configurable, I was looking forward to a dramatic reduction in the sway of programmers, database managers, and anything having to do with operating systems. I was confident that newly minted business process owners would become the centers of information power at client sites and that information technology, while hardly being banished to "the boiler room," would all the same be placed into a proper business support context.

Ah, well.

When business fails to take the lead, we cede SAP to the technologists. And if we leave things up to technologists, nothing will operate, but everything will work. We need to put business behind the SAP wheel.

As you read this book, remember that SAP is no more about information technology than a book is about ink and paper.

It is the client story that matters, and with the ink and paper of SAP, that story can be better written.

This book is organized into roughly three parts. The first covers what went wrong during and after your wedding (the implementation) and getting a handle on how well the marriage (the long-term deployment) is going. The second part of this book provides a blueprint for the ideal organization (Center of Excellence) and how to source that organization in an enlightened fashion. The third part provides details regarding measurement, user competency, business intelligence, and SAP relations. Cafeteria-style reading (i.e. skipping around from chapter to chapter) will not be effective.

Clients pay dearly for implementation mistakes long after the implementation has ended. This chapter identifies the worst of those mistakes and provides an initial direction for correcting them.

1 SAP Marital Counseling: Addressing the Most Common Post-Go-Live Issues

In my work as an industry analyst, I have found that there are a lot of sacred numbers tossed about for which I can seldom find a source. Eighty-twenty rules abound—but why precisely 80-20 rather than 70-30 or 73-27? There was an old saying about how costs for enterprise applications were supposed to be in perfect pie-chart thirds for software, services, and hardware, but I have never found that ratio to be true.

In the late 1990s, one of those sacred numbers was 3.2, as in "clients replace commercial applications, on average, every 3.2 years." While many "sacred numbers" seem dubious, this one, based on my pre-SAP experience (from 1973 to 1995), seems about right.

SAP clearly has a much longer life span than 3.2 years. Back in 2001, I debated with a number of analyst colleagues about the life span of an SAP installation. My first bid of 25 years was met with general derision from analysts with mostly pre-SAP backgrounds, who said "No way. That's way too long." As it happens, there are hundreds of firms that have already marked 20 years or more with SAP. Thousands more will join over the years.

Despite this life span, new SAP clients tend to think short-term, concentrating fully on the implementation project (the wedding) and giving short shrift to the long-term deployment (the marriage).

Many of the post-go-live disappointments can be squarely laid at the doorstep of the implementation project in the vein of "bad wedding, worse marriage." Mark Dendinger, a 15-year SAP project veteran says, "There's a lot of needless pain out there. Not enough clients learn from the mistakes of those who went before them."

Figure 1.1 shows the classic SAP roadmap from proposal to post-honeymoon.

Figure 1.1 The SAP Wedding (SAP Implementation Roadmap)

SAP weddings are often ruined at the outset by a lack of funding. Clients suffer from sticker shock and, worse, will often use pre-SAP project costs as a benchmark. Thus, many projects start out late and over-budget and are carried out with a collective sense of gritted teeth. In such projects, installation predominates at the cost of proper organizational change management, end-user training, and other issues that are erroneously viewed as peripheral.

There are very few SAP divorces (that is, firms dropping SAP in favor of other applications software). Those that we have seen have been the result of a merger rather than a rip and replace. If because of sunk costs alone, firms that adopt SAP are not at all inclined to drop it. The life span of your SAP installation will therefore be in the 20- to 30-year range (see Figure 1.2). If you implemented with little thought in that regard, you may well have set the stage for long-term headaches.

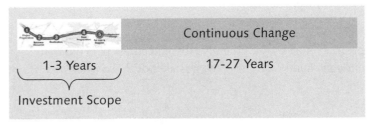

| 1-3 Years | Continuous Change |
| | 17-27 Years |

Investment Scope

Figure 1.2 The SAP Marriage: Life Span of an SAP Implementation

Patrice LeBrun of CGI has been involved in SAP projects for more than a dozen years. He finds that "clients who are adopting SAP have a hard time getting their heads around such a long life span. It isn't until they have had SAP for three or four years that they recognize the extreme long-term nature of it."

I have often debated methodology with leaders of SAP systems integration firms. Across the board, their methodologies include far too little long-term planning of post-implementation considerations. The systems integrators' argument is often that clients are already suffering sticker shock relative to implementation, and the addition of 3% to 5% more time and cost would be a hindrance to closing the deal. ("They'll find out down the line," remarked one morally dubious partner at one of the Usual Suspects).

Faulty implementations can have a negative effect long after the go-live party hangovers have been cured. Table 1.1 summarizes the most common issues faced after SAP go-live.

Issue	Long-Term Effect	Solution
There was no quantifiable measurement of business benefits derived from implementation.	Business leadership has not seen "visible" value of SAP investments.	Value engineering
We had insufficient knowledge transfer.	SAP support staff lack competency and confidence.	Application management assistance or outsourcing
After go-live, we broke up the implementation team and left IT to support the installation.	Business/IT alignment is lost.	SAP Center of Excellence
We shortchanged end-user training due to time or budget limitations.	End users are lacking competency and confidence.	End-user training or SAP Center of Excellence
We over-customized the software rather than adopting inherent business practices.	Software maintenance remains an issue. Business staff cannot configure.	SAP Center of Excellence
We have too many versions or instances to manage, which equals not getting integration as planned.	Application maintenance is a burden and evolution is hindered.	Optimization or reimplementation

Table 1.1 Implementation Issues Affecting Post-Implementation

There are no simple solutions to these issues. However, firms that move in the right direction will lessen their difficulties, just as firms that continue down the same path will merely aggravate them.

Some years ago, I wrote a brief article entitled "Shop Till You Drop at the ERP Mall." It was inspired by research, both primary and experiential, into the ERP-installed base (SAP, PeopleSoft, and Oracle). The research revealed that, after go-live, a large percentage of firms tend to buy more applications software to the detriment of stabilizing their existing ERP platform through business process improvements, end-user training, data synchronization, and the like. In short, rather than addressing the problems listed in the table, many firms merely up the ante.

Software is not an answer to a business question, but instead a variable in an algorithm that can lead to an answer. If you keep driving into a ditch with your car, getting an even faster car only means that you can drive faster into the same ditch. As Dane Anderson, an industry analyst and former consultant, reminds me, "The ditch always wins."

So let's turn our attention to good driving skills that can change the outcome, and let's examine the issues mentioned in Table 1.1 more closely.

Issue	Long-Term Effect	Solution
There was no quantifiable measurement of business benefits derived from implementation.	Business leadership has not seen "visible" value of SAP investments.	Value engineering

Value engineering is the fancy term for working toward goals that have credible business numbers attached. This is the most common issue, and it stems from a failure to view an SAP investment any differently from prior IT investments. Let's face it—before SAP, most IT leaders could justify nearly any investment with some clever spreadsheet work, a few bullet points, and the rallying cry of technical obsolescence. But if your firm is building a new factory or buying out a competitor, you can bet the farm that a complete financial analysis will be prepared. The same should be done for an SAP investment, but here is where the car tends to leave the road and head ominously toward the ditch.

When confronted with a need to measure current performance, most clients respond with one of the following:

- ▶ We don't have the time.
- ▶ We already know things are going to be better, so why bother?
- ▶ We can't agree on KPIs (key performance indicators), or we already have too many.
- ▶ It's not in the budget.
- ▶ The project is already justified.
- ▶ We don't want to know (and/or do not want anyone to see who we really are).

Remember the insurance company CIO I mentioned earlier? Someone high up is going to ask the question, "What did we get out of this investment?" If the only answer you have is "upgraded technology," you might be up the creek without a paddle.

Issue	Long-Term Effect	Solution
We had insufficient knowledge transfer.	SAP support staff lacking competency and confidence	Application management assistance or outsourcing

If in the course of your initial implementation you left the lion's share of SAP configuration to your systems integration partner, the result was certainly a lack of in-house SAP expertise needed to adequately support ongoing business change.

Your options to rectify this include (a) conducting further SAP training for your support staff, (b) hiring more experienced staff, or (c) outsourcing some or all of your applications support. (For more details, see Chapter 4, We Do It Themselves: Outsourcing SAP Applications Support.)

Issue	Long-Term Effect	Solution
After go-live, we broke up the implementation team and left IT to support the installation.	Business/IT alignment is lost.	SAP Center of Excellence

The alignment of business and IT is a sore subject nearly everywhere. For firms that are implementing SAP, it's a great pretext for getting the two together in a common cause.

For too many firms, this project partnership is ephemeral, as the business stakeholders who participate in business blueprinting are thereafter cast adrift and, once live, the SAP installation is solely in the hands of IT. This occurs even in firms that adopt the mantra that SAP is a continuous business endeavor and not a finite IT project. This subject will be addressed in various forms through the remainder of this book.

Issue	Long-Term Effect	Solution
We shortchanged end-user training due to time or budget limitations.	End users are lacking competency and confidence.	End-user training or SAP Center of Excellence

There is one solution that is by far the most effective (and the rarest): Train your users, not only prior to go-live, but also continually thereafter.

This "revelation" came to me in 2002 when I was a speaker at a searchSAP event in London. There were more than 300 attendees, and I asked them to raise their hands if they'd had SAP for three or more years. Nearly all hands went up. I then asked them to keep their hands up if, in the past year, they had provided their end-user base any formal refresher training. All hands went down. After a few seconds, everyone burst into embarrassed laughter.

The joke is on us.

On average, clients invest only 4% to 5% of their implementation budget on training, of which about 50% is dedicated to the end users. The rest goes to the internal project team and to executive awareness. Worse, since end-user training is the penultimate step before go-live and because both budgets and schedules are stretched thin, many clients cheap out and provide foreshortened training. Neutralizing a budget shortfall at the expense of subsequent user competence is a poor trade-off and is usually followed with a hopeful "they'll sort it all out later" attitude.

The result is that users are hesitant, slow, unaware of their role in fulfilling a business process, and perhaps resentful. Since they are at the source of your SAP business process fulfillment, you will have undermined the entire investment.

Wise firms cultivate a culture in which the efficient deployment of SAP applications is constantly reviewed and refined. It is probable that your firm spent 5% or less of its implementation budget on end-user training. It is equally probable that you have no formal budget whatsoever for ongoing training.

Issue	Long-Term Effect	Solution
We over-customized the software rather than adopting inherent business practices.	Software maintenance remains an issue. Business staff cannot configure.	SAP Center of Excellence

For the sake of clarity, a reminder:

▶ Configuring is the setting of business tables that determine the format, the nature, the location, and the destination of information.

▶ Programming is the creation of codes that manipulate the format, the nature, the location, and the destination of information.

Programming, usually done with the ABAP language, represents customization when applied to business applications. Configuration is relatively easy to maintain in comparison to customization. While high levels of customization are increasingly rare, some firms still suffer from customization that is based more upon "personal preference" than actual business requirements that can't be satisfied through configuration.

Issue	Long-Term Effect	Solution
We have too many versions or instances to manage, which equals not getting integration as planned.	Application maintenance is a burden and evolution is hindered.	Optimization or re-implementation

This issue usually arises in undisciplined or poorly organized firms in which reporting lines, authorities, product lines, and/or regional considerations are in conflict.

No discrete action or project can overcome this issue. For the diligent, a long-term consolidation project can occur by which multiple instances are combined into a single instance. For example, a firm with ten disparate instances may consolidate five of them into one, another three into another, and end up with four. Reconciliation or integration across four instances is exponentially simpler than ten.

The large firms I have encountered with more than 200 SAP instances have no real solution other than to implement all over again.

Conclusion

None of the issues explored here are limited to just IT or just business stakeholders. All address both spouses of the SAP marriage, which is why we are using the term "SAP marital counseling." Such counseling should not be characterized by the blame game.

John Ziegler, who was one of the first non-European consultants at SAP America and has as much field experience as any consultant in North America, is surprised when clients blame the software for implementation issues.

"I have been involved with packaged software implementations for the past 20 years," he said. "In all that time, I have never experienced a business application software package that didn't work. That's not to say they have been 'bug-free,' but bugs get caught and fixed. SAP applications software has never been considered buggy. If it was, they wouldn't be in business today."

More clients blame their systems integrators than blame the software. "Clients are so anxious to get to go-live that it is often hard to engage them in conversation about what happens afterward," Mark Dendinger adds. "The best approach is to get them as educated as possible before an implementation project starts. The fallback is to get them educated in the course of the project."

So what about SAP in this regard? As a client, you have SAP software support, an SAP rep anxious to see you buy more software and upgrade regularly, and possibly even SAP Consulting or some other systems integration partner for occasional assistance. As such, SAP is tangential to the long-term deployment and can be called upon for some level of counseling, especially in regard to technical issues, middleware, and training. Improvement in any or all of these areas will vastly improve your situation but will not solve it. Solutions are in your hands.

Whatever issues you are facing, one thing is certain: There are multiple issues, and your various stakeholders don't agree on how to address them. More business intelligence? More applications software? Upgrade? Reduce customization? Train the users? In the next chapter, An SAP Maturity Model, we address how to measure your needs.

The sheer volume of potential activities relative to an installed SAP system can lead to confusion or delusion about what needs to be addressed to improve your SAP maturity. This chapter provides a model that addresses the most crucial elements and provides a visible path to increased maturity and, by extension, better return on investments.

2   An SAP Maturity Model

While the ASAP methodology provides a roadmap to a go-live state and Run SAP provides a roadmap to maintain that state, neither addresses the full dimension of SAP. In this chapter, we explore how firms can lose their way in the early years after go-live and how to emerge from "the SAP woods" onto a clear path for sustainable success.

2.1   Denial, Realization, Determination

Industry analyst firms such as Gartner Inc., Forrester Research, and IDC invest a lot of resources in maturity models regarding enterprise software, hardware, middleware, and the like. The concentration is on the maturity (usability, robustness, flexibility, etc.) of such assets. At a given point, a product or service is deemed "mature," but I seldom see the other necessary arc—that of client maturity—in such a conclusion.

SAP business software and its underlying technology have been generally deemed "mature" since about 2003. But as stated earlier, we estimate that only one in five SAP clients is actually thriving. Needless to say, this observation leads to a belief that widespread client SAP maturity is not yet there.

After go-live, there remain a number of issues that need to be shaken out. The difficulty often lies in the prioritization of activities. Do you consolidate the gains you've made through the implementation of new applications? Push forward with extended applications? Refine end-user competency?

As previously mentioned, much of my research in recent years has suggested that too many firms fall into the "Shop till you drop at the ERP mall" syndrome by which the purchase of more software is intended to address post-implementation issues. The result is that ever more shakeout issues are raised. The lesson here is that applications software alone is not a solution but merely a possibility.

Another finding from that research is that SAP clients tend to follow a pattern of denial, realization, and determination in the first three years after go-live.

Denial is the presumption in the first year after go-live that all will be well once the installation is simply stabilized.

Realization occurs in the second year, as the shake-out continues with no end in sight, that major reorganization and focus are in order.

Determination to seek sounder solutions often takes place in the third year after go-live. It is at this point that a majority of clients understand that their SAP support organization is inadequate. The question thus turns to priorities and directions. What actions are required (and in what order) to improve SAP maturity?

2.2 From Core Implementation to Evolving Center of Excellence

The maturity model presented in this chapter addresses SAP in a complete sense, meaning an SAP installation that embraces most or all of a firm's key enterprise applications. The model will not work as well for firms that are merely using a small subset of SAP software (such as the Financials module) in concert with legacy or "other" applications.

The model was initially developed in 2003 and has been applied at a vast number of firms. It identifies a client's maturity level and, even better, provides a diagnostic to achieve a higher level of maturity. The underlying assumption is that greater SAP maturity will naturally lead to processing simplification, organizational flexibility, and measurable economies.

The model also points to the creation and maintenance of an organization that will sustain whatever maturity is achieved. We refer to this organization as a Center of Excellence. This term has been applied in a variety of ways and therefore requires some qualification.

First, you can name your organization whatever you like. One of the first efficient SAP organizations I studied was at Delta, which dubbed its group the Client Care Center. The beauty of that term was that "client" meant not only passengers (full disclosure: I am a longstanding Delta Gold client) but also all of the Delta employees. Further, the term does not include that label "SAP." SAP is a means, not an end, and sticking those letters into the name of your business support and evolution center will undermine its task. In addition, the organization should not be confused with what is often termed an SAP Competency Center. These centers are software-centric and are focused primarily on software and middleware performance. These issues are a subset of the subject at hand.

Other terms for Centers of Excellence include Strategic Evolution Center, Business Improvement Center, and Business Fulfillment Center. You get the picture.

To avoid confusion across various monikers, we will stick with *Center of Excellence* throughout this book.

In large enterprises, a fully functional Center of Excellence cannot be created in the course of a single project. Successful firms have built Centers of Excellence over a period of time. The best practice is to build this organization throughout the initial SAP implementation, but very few firms have actually done so.

Chapter 3, Building and Sustaining a Center of Excellence, covers how to plan, build, and maintain a Center of Excellence.

The SAP Maturity Model is comprised of five levels of evolution, from the implementation of core applications through the establishment of an evolving Center of Excellence. The maturity model is shown in Table 2.1.

Level		Business/ IT Dynamic	Enterprise Applications	End Users	Value Management
1	Core applications	There is a link between business and IT for configuration updates.	Enterprise applications are not overly customized; core implementation is complete.	Basic end-user training is complete.	Some tangible measures of success are in place.
2	Stable applications	The role of business in applications evolution is defined.	ERP is the backbone of enterprise applications. Interfacing is complete.	End users fulfill functions without excessive help desk use or support.	Business results are tracked through the system.
3	CoE defined	Business has active ownership of business processes. Current KPIs are measured.	The applications portfolio is inventoried.	End users receive periodic refresher training.	KPIs are established for all levels.

Table 2.1 The SAP Maturity Model

Level	Business/ IT Dynamic	Enterprise Applications	End Users	Value Management
4 **CoE managed**	KPI measures and targets are in the system. The Enterprise Program Management Office (EPMO) directs business process transformation.	The applications portfolio has been rationalized.	End users are trained in business processes, and continuous training is in place.	Business process changes are directed by KPI results.
5 **CoE evolving**	Business process change is guided by KPI performance; configuration is in the hands of business.	The applications portfolio has been optimized.	End-user job performance is linked to business process performance.	Business process changes are guided by effective business intelligence.

Table 2.1 The SAP Maturity Model (Cont.)

The focus of this model is on four avenues of pursuit: the business and IT dynamic, enterprise applications, end users, and value management.

Altogether, the model tests 35 best practices, each weighted for importance for each level of maturity. As a result, the activity categories are generally weighted accordingly.

For example, in level 2, stable applications, we test seven best practices. Relatively speaking, we assign a higher importance weight of 17% to "End users are functional" than the 10% importance weight for "Business managers understand their SAP role/responsibilities."

As will be seen, system and applications practices are deemed highly important in the early levels of maturity, while business and value management practices grow in importance as maturity rises.

2.2.1   Level 1: Core Applications

Clients may attain this level only if the core implementation and at least the majority of corresponding geographic rollouts have been completed, the end users have been satisfactorily trained, and no significant amount of continuing application implementation is occurring.

The client has agreed on a combination of processes, lines of business, and geographies to be frozen and hence supported by the Center of Excellence. Clients are advised to take a close look at the level of software customization that has been or is still occurring. High levels of customization will negatively impact their ability to move forward with subsequent upgrades of enterprise software or future enterprise software projects. For the first two maturity levels, SAP is the primary focus since SAP is at the center of the enterprise application portfolio.

2.2.2   Level 2: Stable Applications

Applications stability is a combination of end users being functional, infrastructure being adequate, and the interfacing of enterprise applications to other related applications generally being in place. An application Center of Excellence cannot be adequately defined, staffed, and effective if enterprise operations remain unstable.

2.2.3   Level 3: Center of Excellence Defined

This is the "hump" maturity level in which clients must turn the corner from simply operating the installed applications and move toward an evolutionary state in which the business and the IT groups are better aligned. Certainly, the definition of this alignment can happen much earlier—not only at the business process/data management levels, but also at the end-user level. Further, the client must, in this phase, begin to scroll together all enterprise applications, whether vendor-supplied or in-house/legacy.

We also recommend that the client engage in an application portfolio rationalization exercise. At this stage in the maturity model, a client must have key performance indicators (KPIs) established within systems, including a proper measurement of current actual KPI performance.

2.2.4 Level 4: Center of Excellence Managed

A managed Center of Excellence presumes that end users are aware of their role within business processes. It also presumes that business staff members are actively involved in business process analysis and design, have direct roles in enterprise application configuration (where applicable), or have direct authorization over enterprise application software development. At this point in the maturity model, a balance will be struck between business-oriented staff and IT staff, in which IT professionals are guided by highly focused business decision-makers centered on business process improvement that will yield measurable business results.

2.2.5 Level 5: Center of Excellence Evolving

An evolving Center of Excellence is immediately responsive to business threats or opportunities, with end users fully participating in business performance across business processes. Business processes are continually improved based on key performance indicators (KPIs) and enterprise program management strategies. KPIs are benchmarked. The system indicates which transactions within business processes impact KPIs. Executive decisions to ameliorate KPIs are tracked in a knowledge management system.

2.3   Elements of SAP Maturity

Elements of SAP maturity include best practices in the categories of business and IT dynamics, end-user competency, application maturity, and value management. Without adequate maturity in all these areas, clients will struggle to gain sufficient return on their enterprise application investments.

► **Business and IT dynamic**
An IT organization is intended to drive business results and an effective application Center of Excellence; therefore, it must also be staffed by business personnel. Do not think of this as business and IT alignment, as the word "alignment" suggests that there is a partnership. It is not a partnership. IT is in service to business.

► **Enterprise applications**
The state of the applications (software, functionality, reliability, and interoperability) will have an impact on staff members' ability to impact change (business process improvement). Unstable applications will consume both IT and business resources with support tasks.

► **End users**
End users are the people who actually run the business processes delivered by the enterprise applications. Their level of competence (which is ideally driven by a continuous training program) will have a direct effect on business process performance and a firm's ability to absorb continuous change. Most firms have failed in this regard because of their reliance on end-user training practices that fail to address the extended lifespan of enterprise applications and thus do not include continuous training.

► **Value management**
Value should be measured at the KPI level, and results should be the key drivers to business process improvements. Without value management, business staff will not adequately support a Center of Excellence.

Attaining a new level of maturity requires minimum performance achieved in the best practices for each level. As you will see in Section 2.4, minimum acceptable performance is a 7 on a scale of 1 to 10. Since the importance of individual best practices will vary, we have assigned a relative weight to each (see Table 2.2).

Business/IT Dynamic	Applications	End Users	Value Management
45%	30%	15%	10%

Table 2.2 SAP Maturity Elements

These importance weightings have been used many times, but it is obvious that each client will have different relative weights. The tool I use in helping clients allows them to redistribute weight as necessary, provided, of course, that the total of all relative weights is 100%.

The following paragraphs detail the best practices for each maturity level.

2.3.1   Level 1: Core Applications Implementation

Formation of the enterprise applications Center of Excellence should commence as early as possible in the enterprise SAP lifecycle, but it will not mature unless all elements and practices at this level have been fully addressed.

Table 2.3 shows the maturity best practices for level 1 and their respective weighting.

Best Practice	Weight	Category
We are finished implementing/ rolling out our SAP.	15%	Applications

Table 2.3 Best Practices for Level 1, Core Applications

Best Practice	Weight	Category
Our end users have received SAP training.	10%	End users
We are not adding significant new modules or applications.	15%	Applications
We did not over-customize our applications.	15%	Applications
We have some tangible success measures.	20%	Value management
Our IT staff has been adequately trained to SAP.	15%	Applications
We have a link from business to IT for application updates.	10%	Business/IT dynamic

Table 2.3 Best Practices for Level 1, Core Applications (Cont.)

▶ **We are finished implementing or rolling out our core applications.**

For this element, a firm must have completed its core applications implementations with all minimum interfacing requirements, and its business and IT resources should not be overly committed to ongoing geographic or organizational rollout. In essence, we seek to know to what degree the dust has settled over the implementation effort.

▶ **Our end users have received adequate training.**

End-user training is commonly shortchanged due to budget and time shortfalls. To achieve par for this element, the end-user community must have received sufficient training so it can run basic applications in support of business processes. End users should also be able to run reports, understand parameter choices, and build simple queries.

▶ **We are not adding significant new modules or applications.**

Any efforts to build a viable Center of Excellence will be undermined if the installation suffers instability due to a lack of IT resources. Continuing geographic rollouts or application extensions will hinder a firm's ability to stabilize the application portfolio and thus delay Center of Excellence maturity.

▶ **We did not over-customize our applications.**
If enterprise applications are heavily customized at the major business process level (e.g., orders to cash), IT staff will have a maintenance burden that will inhibit the eventual Center of Excellence when it comes to business process change (not to mention the upgrade difficulties that are in store, since upgrades will not carry all customizations). This element should be scored in relation to both the number and the nature of the customizations made to a firm's software in lieu of standard software configuration.

▶ **We have some tangible success measure.**
At the very least, your organization should have some measurable criteria for core implementation success. The importance of measurement (and value management) rises significantly in subsequent levels of SAP maturity.

▶ **Our IT staff has been adequately trained to application support.**
Normally, in the course of an enterprise application implementation, part of the IT staff is trained in general application principles as well as software configuration. While most firms presume that configuration skills are the key, we consider it imperative for the IT staff to learn business process and integration skills as well. In essence, this element should be scored according to the level of knowledge acquisition made by the IT staff during and after the core implementation.

▶ **We have a link between the business and the IT organization for application updates.**
At an absolute minimum, there should be some communication mechanism between various business entities and the IT staff (or business and IT group) assigned to ongoing software configuration.

2.3.2   Level 2: Stable Applications

As Dane Anderson points out, "One man's stability is another man's chaos." As you will see further on, we address the "subjectivity" issue by involving multiple assessment points of view. Table 2.4 shows the maturity best practices for level 2 and their weighting.

Best Practice	Weight	Category
SAP base is the backbone of our enterprise applications.	12%	Applications
Our end users are functional.	17%	End users
We have sufficient business and IT resources to maintain stability.	15%	Business/IT dynamic
SAP operations are reliable.	15%	Applications
Business managers understand their SAP role/responsibility.	10%	Business/IT dynamic
We do not foresee a major upgrade in less than 10 months.	10%	Applications
We have measures of our current business KPIs.	9%	Value management
Enterprise applications are generally interfaced.	12%	Applications

Table 2.4   Best Practices for Level 2, Stable Applications

▶ **The SAP base is the backbone of our enterprise applications.** Without an SAP backbone, maturity will suffer, since these enterprise applications are at the center of the applications portfolio. Even a partial SAP suite that includes financials, order processing, and material management would suffice. If legacy software is the backbone of enterprise applications, subsequent steps in building a Center of Excellence will be compromised because software configuration skills for Center of Excellence members (rather than programming skills) will have minimum impact.

► **Our end users are functional.**
In a post-training mode, the end users are capable of fulfilling their SAP functions without overwhelming levels of help desk assistance. If more than 25% of help desk trouble tickets are training-related, this area needs attention.

► **We have sufficient IT resources to maintain stability.**
In essence, if a firm is constantly in fire-fighting mode, this score would be low. If, however, IT operations around SAP are generally routine, this should score as a seven or better. We have noticed that firms in their first year of SAP operations tend to score low in this regard since the notion of "sufficient IT resources" is still in question.

► **Application operations are reliable.**
Business and end-user staff members will be primed for evolution only if existing operations are reliable. Reliability presumes a minimum acceptable percentage of uptime, a low level of software failures or bugs, and a sufficient flow of reporting such that the business is not negatively impacted by operations.

► **Business management understands its role in applications.**
Maturity will be limited if business management views the evolution of applications as merely an IT subject, rather than a business performance enabler. However, if business management is aware of how the applications platform drives business processes related to business decisions, greater maturity will be achieved.

► **We do not foresee a major upgrade in fewer than ten months.**
If an upgrade of any key enterprise applications (ERP, CRM, SCM) is pending at this point in a firm's application maturity, it will be difficult to free up the resources required to build a Center of Excellence. It is possible that a major upgrade project

will be combined with the creation of a Center of Excellence — an approach that many firms have taken.

▶ **We have measures of our current KPIs.**
This presumes that (a) the KPIs that will be used to guide Center of Excellence efforts around business process improvement have been identified and (b) current performance in that regard has been measured. The highest possible maturity would result if the firm has also determined industry and peer averages for the same KPIs.

▶ **Enterprise applications are generally interfaced.**
Interfaces (both real-time and batch) between the SAP backbone and other key applications should be complete. The basic measure here is whether significant key interfacing has been completed to such a point that all business applications can operate efficiently.

John Ziegler says, "I visit a lot of clients who claim that their SAP solution is running pretty well, but, after gaining further insight, I find that they have aimed too low. They can keep the SAP lights on but they aren't burning all that brightly."

2.3.3 Level 3: Center of Excellence Defined

If a Center of Excellence is created in the course of an enterprise applications implementation, this level will be attained more quickly than otherwise.

Note that from this point forward, more than half of the remaining best practices (including four of the eight for this level) relate to business and IT dynamics. Creating and maintaining such alignment is a major challenge, as evidenced by the fact that every year of *CIO Magazine's* "State of the CIO" survey lists it as the highest priority.

Best Practice	Weight	Category
We have business-assigned business process ownership.	18%	Business/IT dynamic
End users receive periodic refresher training.	12%	End users
We have a defined sourcing strategy.	12%	Applications
We have inventoried our applications portfolio.	10%	Applications
CoE organization is defined and staffed.	18%	Business/IT dynamic
Senior management sees a CoE as the means to improve results.	16%	Business/IT dynamic
We have targeted measurable KPI improvement.	10%	Value management
Data issues are manageable and do not inhibit progress.	4%	Applications

Table 2.5 Best Practices of Level 3, Center of Excellence Defined

▶ **We have a business-assigned business process ownership.**
If a firm has established active business process ownership at the business level, this should be given a relatively high score. Active ownership presumes that the business people do more than request or approve changes to business processes and that they actually participate in business process re-engineering. In large organizations, such participation can be full-time.

▶ **End users receive periodic refresher training.**
By periodic, we are referring to quarterly or semiannual formal training events or, for individual users or a small group of users, a focused training session. In essence, the goal is to ensure that the end-user base keeps up with changes due to upgrades or business process evolution. This training should, of course, also be extended to new users.

▶ **We have a defined sourcing strategy.**
Various elements of an emerging Center of Excellence are already being outsourced or are targeted for outsourcing, and all of this is reflected in an established strategy.

▶ **We have inventoried our application portfolio.**
Inevitably, the Center of Excellence will embrace all enterprise applications. Thus, at minimum, a firm must have a complete inventory of all applications, including application name, function, interfaces, number of users, and applications to be included in the Center of Excellence. The end game of this inventory is the identification of all applications to be included in the Center of Excellence and, of great consequence, those destined for retirement.

▶ **Center of Excellence organization, roles, communication channels, and charter are defined.**
A complete blueprint of the enterprise applications Center of Excellence has been established and agreed upon by both business and IT entities, including the purpose and goals of the Center of Excellence, roles of each group, communication and reporting channels, and (where applicable) budgets.

▶ **Senior management sees a Center of Excellence as the means to improve results.**
Senior management recognizes that the highest priority of the Center of Excellence is business process improvement (through which business performance, as reflected in the P&L, will be enhanced). Therefore, senior management has chartered the Center of Excellence to be a business performance driver and not just an IT management organization.

▶ **We have targeted measurable KPI improvement.**
Improvements to key performance indicators are targeted (based on peer and industry comparisons and the firm's strategy), and the business processes affecting those KPIs are identified (online to decision-makers).

▶ **Data issues are manageable and do not inhibit progress.**
Data synchronization across enterprise applications, whether

packaged or legacy, is sufficient to provide flow-through of reporting and successful completion of key business processes.

2.3.4 Level 4: Center of Excellence Managed

Later, in Section 3.10, we will address some of the impediments faced by firms attempting to maintain a workable Center of Excellence. This is the level at which those impediments tend to appear as an organization shifts to a direct business focus.

Best Practice	Weight	Category
Business staff works directly with configuration staff.	15%	Business/IT dynamic
End users are trained to business process roles.	15%	End users
EPMO directs major business process change priorities.	15%	Business/IT dynamic
End-user ecosystem (training/help desk) is sound.	20%	End users
Outsourcing governance is effectively in place.	15%	Business/IT dynamic
Business process changes are directed by KPI results.	10%	Value management
Our applications portfolio has been rationalized.	10%	Applications

Table 2.6 Best Practices of Level 4, Center of Excellence Managed

▶ **Business staff works directly with IT staff on configurations.**
The business staff is fully involved in continuous business process improvement and works in concert with the IT staff to put into effect the software configuration intended to reflect process improvements.

▶ **End users are trained to business process roles.**
End users understand not only system navigation, features, and functions necessary to fulfill their tasks, but also their individual roles in fulfilling business processes, as well as the business benefits that are derived from successful business process completion.

▶ **The Enterprise Program Management Office (EPMO) directs major business process change priorities.**
Through directives from senior leadership, the EPMO collaborates with the business process owners regarding major business process changes based on enterprise initiatives and opportunities.

▶ **End-user ecosystem (training and help desk) is sound.**
A lack of end-user competency will undermine business process efficiency. End users should have a thriving ecosystem. This includes an efficient help desk, super-user support, and sufficient training assets.

▶ **Outsourcing governance is effectively in place.**
Firm governance of outsourcing providers is supported by necessary reviews as well as cost and quality controls.

▶ **Business process changes are directed by KPI results.**
The business process owners closely monitor KPIs. Results provide direction for continuing business process improvement that can be enabled through changes to the enterprise software configuration.

▶ **The application portfolio has been rationalized.**
Redundant and non-strategic applications have been retired, and there is a clear vision for achieving a future state through the enterprise application portfolio. Just getting to this point is, for many firms, a massive undertaking, since eliminating redundant applications can become a political nightmare.

2.3.5   Level 5: Evolving Center of Excellence

While I have found several excellent organizations in the course of my research and consulting, I have never seen a firm fully attain this level. That is simply a matter of "our reach exceeding our grasp." The stumbling points for even the most effective organizations tend to be:

1. Ineffective business measurement
2. An inability to link end-user performance to business process performance

Table 2.7 shows the best practices of this highest level.

Best Practice	Weight	Category
Business staff configures SAP/enterprise applications.	18%	Business/IT dynamic
End-user performance is linked to business process performance.	20%	End users
Business process changes are guided by effective business intelligence.	20%	Value management
Business processes are continually reviewed and improved.	20%	Business/IT dynamic
Our applications portfolio has been optimized.	12%	Applications
Outsource supports are highly effective.	10%	Applications

Table 2.7   Best Practices of Level 5, Evolving Center of Excellence

▶ **Business staff configures SAP/enterprise applications.**
Based on business process redesign, an application management team comprised of primarily business staff does the following: (a) designs non-customized changes to application software; (b) provides functional specifications to the custom application engineers; (c) unit-tests software changes; and (d)

ensures continuous updates to documentation and education to the end-user base.

▶ **End-user performance is linked to business process performance.**
At this stage, with end users already trained in one or more business processes, the client can monitor their performance not only in terms of the fulfillment of business functions, but also in terms of contribution to workflow and business process fulfillment. Ideally, such performance monitoring will be linked to career evaluation, bonus plans, and the like.

▶ **Business process changes are guided by effective business intelligence.**
Beyond KPIs, business process owners have a wide view of business results, including operational, historic, analytic, and predictive data. This intelligence guides the direction for continuing business process improvement, which can be enabled by changes to the enterprise software configuration.

▶ **Business processes are continually reviewed and improved.**
The Center of Excellence reacts to business change/opportunity by reviewing and improving business processes on a regular basis, thus supporting continuous business improvement.

▶ **The application portfolio has been optimized.**
The enterprise application portfolio includes only non-redundant applications that can be managed by the Center of Excellence staff without undue complexity or challenges.

▶ **Outsource supports are highly effective.**
Outsource provider performance is reliable and effective without imposing an unwieldy cost on the enterprise.

So where is your organization in regard to this model? It is important to understand there is no single "You are here." Some firms are more mature in regard to the state of their end users than they are in regard to their value management.

But how do you know? Simple observation will not suffice. If you simply ask various of your stakeholders, it is certain that opinions will vary—and sometimes wildly so. In the next section we provide advice based on long experience as to the best ways to effectively assess your SAP maturity and reveal the diagnostics for improving that maturity.

2.4 Assessing Your SAP Maturity

Because they necessarily entail judgment, assessments can be slippery business. Who assesses what, according to which criteria, and with what underlying knowledge and experience?

Formal assessments tend to consist of a visit from the outside in the form of an analyst or consultant (or multiples thereof). With or without a clipboard, said consultant will question several business stakeholders, SAP support staff, and end users, sift through this input, and return with a verdict (otherwise known as recommendations).

Often the consultant will follow interview scripts. This refinement beats the pants off a general and meandering Q&A session, but organizational reality can often dispassionately slip through the net of a standard query script if the consultant "didn't ask the right questions."

Shortly after I developed the SAP Maturity Model, I seized upon a simpler method that combines "script" with "organizational context." The method presumes what James Surowiecki terms "the wisdom of crowds." While one or two or three of your people will have a strong handle on "what is wrong" with your SAP solution, individual opinions will diverge and consensus may be elusive.

In this application of the wisdom of crowds, I advise polling a good cross-section of business and IT stakeholders in regard to your adherence to the best practices included in the maturity model.

In the proprietary tool that I have been using since 2003, we usually have about 25 to 40 respondents who anonymously score their agreement or disagreement to their company's adherence to each best practice. The scoring scale runs from 10 (absolute and confirmed agreement) to 1 (absolute and confirmed disagreement). Companies are not democracies, so we provide a response weight to each respondent. Thus, in a field of 25 respondents, an individual with broad authority over business process design may have a response weight of 10%, while a Basis administrator (with a lesser purview) will have a response weight of 2%.

We then score as follows:

Rating × Respondent weight × Best practice weight = Result

Note that while respondents are weighted, we also relatively weight the importance of each best practice within a level to a total of 100%. This can be seen in Figure 2.1, wherein the best practice "Our end users are functional" has an importance weight of 17%, whereas "We have measures of our current KPIs" has an importance weight of only 9%.

Any group result less than seven denotes a probable lack of maturity. Any group result less than six describes a problem. Any group result less than five suggests that you should heave something heavy out the window.

It is a good practice to remove the outlier respondents—those who are either too sunny-side up (all nines or tens) or too gloom and doom (all ones or twos).

Figure 2.1 shows a typical example of an assessment for level 2, stable applications.

In the Overall Result column, we provide words rather than simply the score. For example, the result that "SAP is generally the backbone" is based on a score of 6.96. Where we find that the "management role requires attention," it is because the score is 5.85 (which is less than the equivalent of "general agreement").

Stable Applications			Overall Result	
	Statement	Import Weight	Result	Issue
1	SAP base is the backbone of our enterprise applications.	12%	SAP is generally the base bone.	No
2	Our end users are functional.	17%	End users need more SAP competence.	Yes
3	We have sufficient IT resource to maintain stability.	15%	IT resource needs attention.	Yes
4	SAP operations are reliable.	15%	SAP operations are satisfactory.	No
5	Business managers understand their SAP role/responsibility.	10%	Management role requires attention.	Yes
6	We do not foresee a major upgrade in less than 10 months	10%	Stability will not be affected by a major upgrade.	No
7	We have measures of our current business KPIs.	9%	Current KPI measurement is excellent.	No
8	Enterprise applications are generally interfaced.	12%	Interfaces are generally sufficient.	No
		100%		

Category Result			Overall Diagnostic	
Category	Diagnostic		Result	6.92
End Users	Energetically address shortfalls		Level Attainment	Shortfall
Business/IT Alignment	Energetically address shortfalls		Margin	-1.08
Value Management	Strong SAP maturity element		Advise more effort to fully stabilize	
Applications	Nearly mature in this category			

Figure 2.1 Example: Assessment for Level 2, Stable Applications

The diagnostic for this level of maturity is fairly clear, as there are three results that beg attention:

▶ End users need more SAP competence.

▶ IT resources require attention.

▶ Management role requires attention.

The tool has other features, including an analysis of the difference in response between various groups (e.g., business vs. IT, one site vs. another, or management vs. line staff). We long ago noted, for example, that business respondents invariably assign lower scores than do IT respondents. The level of the response difference is a diagnostic of specific subjects of disagreement and how severe the level of disagreement is.

General maturity (an overall score) is not entirely cogent. What matters is maturity by category of effort.

Since business stakeholders and IT staff tend to see things from entirely different perspectives, it is advised to measure the alignment or lack thereof between the group responses. In the example matrix in Figure 2.2, we find a severe misalignment in regard to the applications portfolio.

Center of Excellence Defined		Group Analysis	
Statement	Import Weight	IT	Business
		45%	50%
1 We have business-assigned BP ownership.	20%	Fair response alignment	
2 End users receive periodic refresher training.	12%	Excellent response alignment	
3 We have measures of our current KPIs.	15%	Group misalignment	
4 We have inventoried our application portfolio.	10%	Severe misalignment	
5 CoE organization is defined and staffed.	20%	Excellent response alignment	
6 Senior management sees a CoE as the means to improve results.	16%	Slight misalignment	
7 Our SAP infrastructure is flexible.	3%	Excellent response alignment	
8 We have an acceptable level of data synchronization.	4%	Excellent response alignment	
	100%		

Figure 2.2 Measuring Alignment of Response Between Groups

A comparison of totals by category against an expected "par" reveals what subjects need most to be addressed. In this example, that is "Business/IT Dynamic" (see Figure 2.3).

An assessment of this sort is not intended to be the final word about your agenda. However, it provides a crucial "group consensus" bottom line in regard to the direction that an agenda should take.

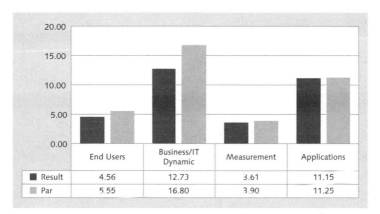

	End Users	Business/IT Dynamic	Measurement	Applications
■ Result	4.56	12.73	3.61	11.15
▨ Par	5.55	16.80	3.90	11.25

Figure 2.3 SAP Maturity Categories

Collective input provides greater credibility than does the input of one external "guru." I learned this once and for all while working as a lead advisor to a branch of the Defense Department when I was concerned that my clients were lacking sufficient SAP knowledge to launch their very ambitious project. My recommendation was a two-day SAP seminar, which they declined on the premise that they were up to speed. "We've met with systems integrators and other vendors, and we've all read *The SAP Blue Book*," they said. "We're all set."

To test this premise, they agreed to an SAP Engagement Readiness Assessment that works in the same fashion as the maturity assessment described in this chapter. The levels of readiness tested are for the strategic profile, organizational profile, goals and measurements, consulting/education, and awareness and commitment. The results of this assessment were disappointing to the colonels and resulted in a major conference, during which one man angrily stated, "I couldn't care less what Michael Doane says. I know we're ready!"

I reminded the audience that it wasn't I who was asserting that they weren't ready, saying, "It's seventy-five of your own people, including most of you." They were convinced enough to invest some time and money to address the diagnostic. If I had been telling them and I'd been basing my opinion on a more traditional assessment, I doubt I could have won them over.

How formally or informally you assess your SAP maturity is, of course, entirely up to you. In that light, here are some observations based on dozens of such assessments over the past five years:

▶ Very few firms have a handle on business measurement, let alone business measurement at the KPI level.

▶ The area of lesser concern tends to be the state of the enterprise applications. That is because most firms concentrate the majority of their resources on this subject. The business and IT dynamic is difficult to attain and even more difficult to maintain.

▶ End users always get the short end of the budget stick.

2.5 Best Practices for Evolving to a Mature Center of Excellence

Clients that have already implemented enterprise applications and are seeking to improve Center of Excellence maturity should address the individual categories that need improvement and seek to coordinate their relative progress.

Enterprise application issues predominate early in the maturity model (evels 1 and 2), while business and IT dynamic issues come to the fore in levels 3 through 5. Below, we take a cross-sectional view of maturity and consider it from a variety of perspectives (e.g., end user and business process).

Clients are advised to address these categories as Center of Excellence-building activities rather than attempt to move progressively from level to level. Details regarding the "how to" of the practices are included in Chapter 3, Building and Sustaining a Center of Excellence.

2.5.1 End-User Maturity

End-user maturity follows a simple arc from initial training to business process "ownership" (see Table 2.8). Firms have been challenged to fulfill the remaining steps due to a lack of ownership or budget for continuous training and an inability to link end-user competency to business process performance.

Level	End Users
1	Our end users have received SAP training.
2	Our end users are functional.
3	End users receive periodic refresher training.
4	End users are trained to business process roles.
4	The end-user ecosystem (training/help desk) is sound.
5	End-user performance is linked to business process performance.

Table 2.8 Levels of End-User Maturity

Levels 1, 2, and 3 should be directly addressed during initial user training.

Patrice LeBrun of CGI notes, "Clients tend to be surprised at how low they score in this regard. End users are seldom on their radar, and the revelation of their neglect in this regard is noteworthy."

2.5.2 Business and IT Dynamic Maturity

When it comes to the business and IT dynamic, the stumbling block for most firms is the measurement and tracking of KPIs as business performance measurement is sought through other means or neglected altogether. Further, firms have shown a tendency to achieve a "to-be" state and then cease to evolve. Maturity regarding business and alignment requires a continual refresh of the to-be vision that should be provided by the Enterprise Program Management Office (EPMO) in conjunction with the business process owners.

If you do not have an EPMO or the equivalent, you will need another means to generate, define, and pursue continually refreshed to-be visions.

Level	Business/IT Dynamic
1	We have a link from the business to IT for application updates.
2	We have sufficient business and IT resources to maintain stability.
2	Business managers understand their SAP role/responsibility.
3	We have business-assigned business process ownership.
3	CoE organization is defined and staffed.
3	Senior management sees a CoE as the means to improve results.
4	Business staff works directly with configuration staff.
4	The EPMO directs major business process change priorities.
4	Outsourcing governance is effectively in place.
5	Business staff configures SAP/enterprise applications.
5	Business processes are continually reviewed and improved.

Table 2.9 Levels of Business/IT Dynamic Maturity

2.5.3 Enterprise Applications Maturity

A Center of Excellence cannot be established until the applications are stable and rationalized. This usually begins with SAP, which is at the center of the application portfolio.

Level	Enterprise Applications
1	We are finished implementing/rolling out our SAP solution.
1	We are not adding significant new modules or applications.

Table 2.10 Levels of Enterprise Applications Maturity

Level	Enterprise Applications
1	We did not over-customize our applications.
1	Our IT staff has been adequately trained in SAP.
2	SAP base is the backbone of our enterprise applications.
2	SAP operations are reliable.
2	We do not foresee a major upgrade in less than 10 months.
2	Enterprise applications are generally interfaced.
3	We have a defined sourcing strategy.
3	We have inventoried our applications portfolio.
3	Data issues are manageable and do not inhibit progress.
4	Our applications portfolio has been rationalized.
5	Our applications portfolio has been optimized.
5	Outsource supports are highly effective.

Table 2.10 Levels of Enterprise Applications Maturity (Cont.)

2.5.4 Value Management Maturity

This category has proven to be the most challenging due to a chronic inability of business and IT to come together. Only when IT accepts itself as being in service to business, and when business stakeholders take an active role in business intelligence and business process improvement, will value management take root.

Level	Value Management
1	We have some tangible success measures.
2	We have measures of our current business KPIs.
3	We have targeted measurable KPI improvement.

Table 2.11 Levels of Value Management Maturity

Level	Value Management
4	Business process changes are directed by KPI results.
5	Business process changes are guided by effective business intelligence.

Table 2.11 Levels of Value Management Maturity (Cont.)

2.6 The Overriding Importance of a Rational Business/IT Dynamic

Management of the SAP lifecycle is clearly not the realm of IT alone. Most clients are required to significantly alter their point of view to mature in this regard.

Throughout the maturation of a Center of Excellence, the business/IT dynamic rises in importance (see Table 2.12).

Maturity Level	# of Best Practices	Related to Business/ IT Dynamic	Percentage
1: Core implementation	7	1	14%
2: Stability	8	2	25%
3: CoE defined	8	2	25%
4: CoE managed	7	2	29%
5: CoE evolving	6	2	33%

Table 2.12 The Importance of the Business/IT Dynamic Rises as Does SAP Maturity

The following are three barriers to this alignment:

1. Business personnel's understandable refusal to be viewed as IT
2. A chronic failure to measure the business benefits of IT
3. The break-up of implementation teams after go-live

To address the first barrier, be aware that language matters, and IT language is a business-killer. Firms that successfully align business and IT tend to have organizations with neutral or business-centric monikers like Customer Care Center, Center of Excellence, or Center for Advanced Business. Such organizations may have technical IT staff around, but the ambiance is strictly business.

Brian Dahill, who has spent many years helping clients build Centers of Excellence, leans toward a straightforward viewpoint. "Too often IT is cited as the reason for business objectives not being met. They aren't 'fast' enough, they 'cost too much.' In reality, many business leaders don't want to collaborate with IT on a functional level. Some fail to see the value of business-centric approach and need to be educated. But a few simply want to continue to use IT as a scapegoat for failing to achieve their goals."

The second barrier exists because many enterprise applications organizations are driven by a bullet-point vision that does not provide business focus. A failure to target and track business benefits during implementation usually leads to continuing failure to measure after go-live. If KPIs are tracked, business staff will be more inclined to participate in a Center of Excellence.

In a great majority of enterprise application implementations, business people are brought into the team for a finite period, with a goal of completing business process design and configuration. Nearly all of the enterprise application implementation methodologies presume that this activity will occur once (as clients seek to move from as-is to to-be). Without a plan of continuous business improvement, clients revert to the pre-project mode in which business people request and negotiate IT changes rather than actively participate in those changes.

We strongly recommend that clients keep their teams largely intact, albeit at lower staff levels, after go-live.

Massive investments in enterprise applications are intended to result in even more massive business benefits. While most firms have shown some success in this area, few firms are taking full advantage of their enterprise application assets. While incremental improvements to any of the four key categories (stabilizing the applications, improving end-user competency, adding in some reports with measures, and realigning the business with the IT organization) are welcome, only a concerted effort along all four axes will result in acceptable enterprise application maturity.

Measuring your maturity is a prerequisite for improving your maturity. In the next chapter, we provide insight into the best means possible for doing so: by establishing a sustainable Center of Excellence.

Success with SAP is best furthered by having a sustainable organization by which the return on SAP assets can be maximized. Such an organization will necessarily be business-centric.

3 Building and Sustaining a Center of Excellence

After implementing SAP software, clients should continue to fulfill most of the activities included in the implementation project, if on a different scale. That means a continuous refresh of the "to-be" vision and continuous business process blueprinting and change.

3.1 New Lifecycle

While the focus of this chapter is the management and maturation of SAP business applications through a continuous lifecycle, we will include legacy applications. These are defined as applications that were specifically developed for a client, either in-house or through contractual application development as opposed to SAP applications such as Enterprise Resource Planning (SAP ERP), Customer Relationship Management (CRM), and Supply Chain Management (SCM).

Therefore, the Center of Excellence, if fully extended, should embrace all enterprise applications.

Since the first great wave of SAP implementations in the 1990s, the necessity and complexity of managing an SAP lifecycle have continued to grow as both the breadth and depth of business functionality have risen exponentially. The vast majority of SAP clients have interfaced these applications to retained legacy systems, which complicates lifecycle management because these applications have different lifecycles.

3.1.1 The Legacy Applications Lifecycle

Legacy applications are built and maintained through programming and have a higher degree of obsolescence than packaged applications. This applies to both fully custom-built applications and packaged applications that have been, through time, heavily customized to the point that they require programming maintenance similar to custom applications.

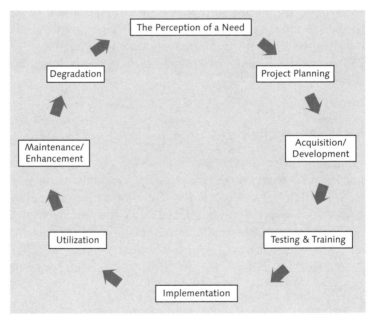

Figure 3.1 The Legacy Applications Lifecycle

Figure 3.1 shows the typical lifecycle of a legacy application. This cycle applies not only to the initial development of a custom application, but also to subsequent application extensions, revisions, patches, and interfaces.

Application degradation occurs when the application no longer serves the business, the underlying technology of the application becomes obsolete, or both. Vertical applications that are interfaced to other vertical applications tend to have a shorter lifespan than do horizontal, business process-based applications. For example, a custom-built sales order processing application that is interfaced to disparate accounting, procurement, and production planning applications is more likely to be replaced than a sales order processing application that is part of a suite that fulfills the orders to cash (OTC) business process.

Prior to the rise of software firms such as SAP, Oracle, PeopleSoft, J.D. Edwards, and Siebel in the 1990s, few software vendors were retained by clients for more than five years running, with the notable exceptions of American Software, Computer Associates, and SAS. The life span of most business applications through the 1980s was between three and six years, as technological shifts such as distributive processing and the increasing relevance of the personal computer led clients to rip and replace.

The Y2K debacle fueled this activity and drove many clients to ERP, since in many cases the cost of such acquisition proved to be marginally more expensive than a Y2K fix.

3.1.2 The SAP Applications Lifecycle

Enterprise applications have long since proven to have a much longer life span than legacy applications. This is the result of two key drivers:

1. The sunk-cost investments made by clients when moving to enterprise applications software are of such importance that abandonment after implementation is scarcely conceivable.

2. The critical mass, in terms of resources, revenues, and growth rate, of major software vendors such as SAP and Oracle has led to a continuous stream of upgrades and application extensions, often negating the need for a client to enhance the soft-

ware with in-house IT staff. This second point also leads to additional sunk costs.

As noted earlier, many companies have had SAP software for more than 25 years, having implemented R/2 in the 1980s, upgraded to R/3 in the 1990s, and upgraded to newer versions since the onset of the new millennium. Thus, there is no "obsolete" point in the SAP lifecycle (see Figure 3.2).

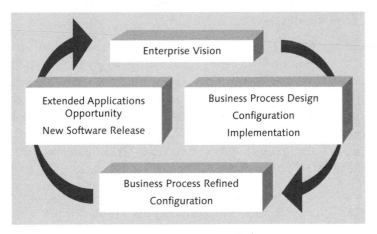

Figure 3.2 Continuous Business Improvement Cycle

In the following sections, we will explore the challenges and best practices for managing and maturing the SAP lifecycle for a client with core enterprise and legacy applications.

The applications portfolio is necessarily centered on ERP (see Figure 3.3). Therefore, successful SAP lifecycle management must depend on a high level of SAP ERP integration.

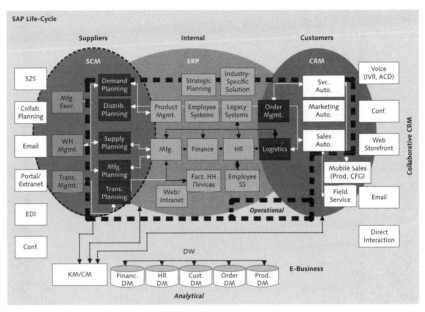

Figure 3.3 Typical Applications Portfolio, Centered on ERP

3.2 Pre-SAP Implementation Strategies and Best Practices

Clients move to enterprise applications for a variety of reasons, but the two most overriding benefits of enterprise applications are data integration and consolidation at all levels. The reduction of labor and of redundancy, the flexibility of process change, a high level of data integrity, and ease of reporting can be derived if data integration and consolidation at all levels are achieved.

It is a fact, however, that a large percentage of enterprise applications clients fail to adequately achieve data integration and consolidation. What they have in common, beyond implementation mistakes, is a failure to make the move from legacy to enterprise applications with sufficient foreknowledge and strategy. In this section, we will cover the key strategic areas that must be addressed in a disciplined fashion.

3.2.1 Data Migration/Manifest Planning

Enterprise applications implementation methodologies tend to include data migration and data manifest in a phase after blueprinting and software configuration. Given the importance of this subject, we believe data migration and data manifest planning should occur even prior to software selection, especially for large-scale enterprise applications endeavors.

Key master files for any enterprise applications installation are those for clients, suppliers, and materials. As clients migrate data from legacy systems to enterprise applications, two key obstacles arise:

1. Multiple records exist for the same item and require data cleansing.

2. Master records will not be complete, since enterprise applications master files include considerably more information than legacy master files, which leads to data manifest efforts.

The latter obstacle is especially important in that the tight integration of enterprise applications software requires that key master file fields be populated, or functionality will not be possible.

As master file volume rises, these obstacles can become nightmarish, and clearly the materials master is the most daunting.

Much of the data cleansing can be done through automated means, but don't underestimate the effort required to migrate data from legacy to enterprise applications. One Fortune 100 firm estimated that the effort to successfully migrate 400,000 material master records from diverse legacy systems to SAP took five people years, with the majority of this effort being given over to data manifest.

3.2.2   Instance, Version, and Data Center Management Planning

Large-scale enterprise applications installations, with very large user bases, generally extend across multiple geographies, each of which is implemented at different times. There is no "big bang" large-scale implementation.

The long-term maintenance of common standards and coherent data can be jeopardized in three ways:

1. Multiple instances or versions are implemented within the same overall installation.

2. Too many data centers are deployed.

3. The software is heavily customized.

In this section, we will concentrate on instances, versions, and data centers.

When client sites are implemented (in a geographic roll-out) at a time quite disparate from initial site implementation, it is probable that the enterprise applications vendor has issued upgrades. Thus, site number 15 may be inclined to implement the new version to avoid a consequent upgrade program. However, if the preceding 14 sites are working on a prior version, such a choice may not be optimal since version differences may be important.

Varying instances or versions can also occur when parts of the client organization resist adopting data hierarchies or business processes (or both) that have been established at other sites. Instead, new versions or instances are established that, in essence, need to be interfaced to "brother" enterprise applications installations. As these variations proliferate, data coherency declines.

In the case of SAP, for example, it is often advised that clients should not have more than three separate instances, yet countless large organizations have more than 100 and cannot consolidate data across the whole.

One of my clients has more than 200 instances. Some years ago, they put out a request for proposal to all the top SAP systems integration firms asking for help in reducing that number from more than 200 to less than 30 instances. None of the firms even responded, as the task was deemed impossible.

By the same token, when data centers proliferate beyond two or three, data maintenance becomes more onerous. A foundational point of enterprise applications is the existence of a single database for all integrated applications. Thus, in a large organization, master data management is an exceptional challenge that is only further complicated as data centers proliferate.

Table 3.1 illustrates how catering to local or specific concerns will degrade integration across the whole of enterprise applications. When beginning with a highly centralized organization and moving down the spectrum of less centralized organizations to a highly decentralized organization, the results for differing criteria will change.

In the example, local business flexibility and process flexibility are deemed less important than process integration and cost reduction, for example. Thus, the relative integration is higher when the organization is centralized.

While a fully centralized enterprise applications plant may not be viable, organizations need to establish and maintain a tolerance level that balances individual unit requirements against the imperative for continued integration and consolidation capability.

Model	Centralized			Less Centralized		Hubbed		Decentralized	
Criteria	Import	Means	Score	Means	Score	Means	Score	Means	Score
Process integration	5	5	25	3	15	2	10	1	5
Process cost reduction	5	4	20	3	15	1	5	1	5
Lowest costs	4	5	20	4	16	2	8	2	8
Local business flexibility	3	2	6	4	12	4	12	5	15
Process flexibility	3	4	12	3	9	3	9	2	6
Legacy retirement	3	1	3	3	9	3	9	4	12
Relative integration			**86**		**76**		**53**		**51**

Table 3.1 Decrease of Integration from Centralized to Decentralized Systems

3.2.3 Application Portfolio Management

The failure to energetically retire legacy systems will leave an organization with an unnecessary burden of software maintenance for those systems and probable interfacing maintenance to the core enterprise applications.

While clients move to enterprise applications with the intention of replacing legacy systems, the market is rife with clients that fail to adequately retire legacy systems after enterprise applications go live. This occurs primarily because of:

► Resistance on the part of stakeholders to conform to newly adopted processes; such resistance is frequently due to legacy functionality that stakeholders feel they cannot do without and that cannot be reproduced with enterprise applications.

► The failure of an organization to adequately plan and implement legacy retirement.

► The failure of an organization to adequately train end users to enterprise applications; as a consequence, end users will continue to use legacy software if it is still available.

► The often erroneous "not invented here" notion that because a legacy system is customized to a firm's existing processes it is, by definition, a better fit.

A legacy retirement plan should take into account what legacy applications will be retired as of the initial enterprise applications implementation. Many organizations succeed to this point but falter through the initial implementation for the reasons cited above.

Where organizations fail most often is after the initial implementation, when momentum cannot be sustained. The plan should also be extended to include subsequent legacy retirement that will occur when (a) extended applications are implemented and/ or (b) when extended functionality can be derived with existing applications (either through configuration or customization).

3.3   Why Firms Need a Center of Excellence

After going live with SAP applications, many client firms struggle through operational issues. Business performance often takes a back seat to day-to-day applications management.

The fact is, too few implementing firms properly plan for post-go-live operations and fail to refresh their to-be vision. As a result, they are not prepared to seize measurable business benefit from their SAP investment.

A key element of the new business and IT dynamic is the ability of a client to gain continuous business improvement rather than the incremental gains afforded by the traditional business and IT dynamic (see Figure 3.4).

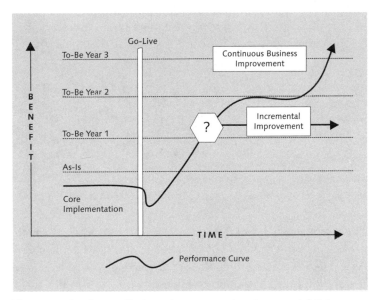

Figure 3.4 Continuous Business Improvement vs. Incremental Gains

The full solution to this "as-is rut" is the creation of a Center of Excellence with the following goals in mind:

▶ An optimization of business processes that drive business benefit continually

▶ An optimization of end-user competency and employee fulfillment of business processes

▶ Continued coherence and integration of functionality and data through all process chains

Figure 3.5 illustrates the relationship between business and to-be as well as the relationship between IT and as-is. It is up to business to drive the vision and IT to support it.

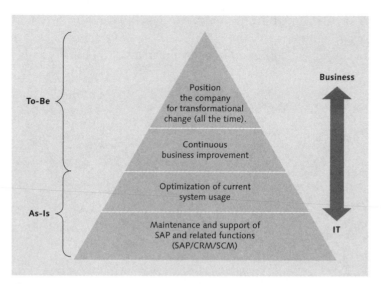

Figure 3.5 As-Is Activities Are Static; To-Be Activities Are Evolutionary

The essential purpose of the Center of Excellence is to drive applications maturity and increase effective applications deployment. As detailed in the preceding chapter, applications are not deemed mature until their evolution is guided by business results (read: business metrics).

The key organizational difference for a client firm moving to a Center of Excellence is the shift of some traditional IT functions into the Center of Excellence, including business process design, integration management, and enterprise applications business functional configuration and programming.

3.4 Center of Excellence Organization

Among the successful Centers of Excellence I have seen over many years, no two are identical in terms of organization.

What they do have in common are these key characteristics:

▶ Clear lines of communication and authority

▶ Well-defined roles within the Center of Excellence

▶ Intrinsic business and IT alignment in which business predominates and IT serves

The organization described in Figure 3.6 is a base template that will vary according to your firm's size, geographic reach, and applications portfolio. Later in this chapter (Section 3.7) we provide some variant templates.

Note that the Center of Excellence resides outside the traditional IT organization. In this sample positioning, it is presumed that the CIO is a "change agent" rather than merely a senior IT official.

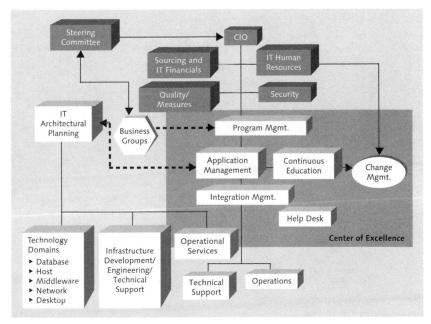

Figure 3.6 Base Template for Positioning the Center of Excellence Within an Organization

There is nothing especially technical about the Center of Excellence: Application management is driven by the lines of business via program management, and in turn, application management drives continuous education, change management, and integration management.

Further, application management provides input to IT leadership where infrastructure, database, middleware, and the like are affected.

The Center of Excellence is organized as shown in Figure 3.7.

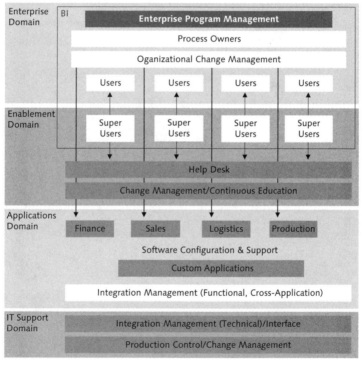

Figure 3.7 Center of Excellence Organization

Note that the super users are, understandably, in both the enterprise and enablement domains. Also note that business intelligence is entirely in the realm of business. We'll discuss this subject more in Chapter 7, Intelligent Business Intelligence.

This organization does not have to be housed in the same office or even in the same location. There are untold variations of virtual Centers of Excellence.

Many firms outsource the application and support domains either in whole or in part on the premise that these domains are less strategic than the enterprise and enablement domains. This option is covered in separate chapters of this book.

There are four "domains" that comprise an enterprise applications Center of Excellence:

▶ Enterprise domain: defines how programs and processes are managed and fulfilled

▶ Enablement domain: defines how end users are prepared and supported

▶ Application domain: defines how applications are configured and integrated

▶ IT support domain: defines how integrated applications are maintained and supported

These domains are not discrete or closed-end organizations. Each has some level of interaction with the others, the only exception being that there is no interaction between the enterprise and IT support domains.

3.4.1 Enterprise Domain

The Center of Excellence is run by the Enterprise Program Management Office (EPMO) or equivalent, which reports to the CIO (or designated change agent) and the IT steering committee while receiving its project initiatives from the various business lines. The EPMO drives the vision, strategy, budget, and prioritization for application management:

▶ Formal software implementation projects

▶ Directives for specific business process changes or improvements

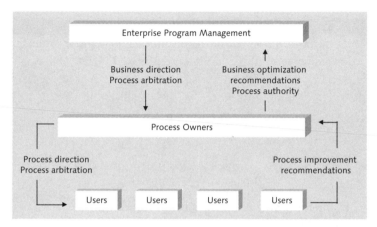

Figure 3.8 Enterprise Domain: Defining Program and Process Planning and Management

Ideally, these initiatives will be driven by KPIs and traditional business imperatives such as mergers, organizational changes, and event-driven programs. In essence, the EPMO is responsible for an evolving to-be vision.

If your firm does not have an official EPMO, the role we have defined here can simply be fulfilled by top management.

However, the EPMO also manages the enterprise applications portfolio, standards, and measures and sub-manages high-level vendor relationships. These responsibilities may not be carried out by top management.

Process owners address implementation and process issues across lines of business and take direction from the CIO (or designated change agent) and the EPMO. Their primary function is to drive continual business process improvements targeting KPIs.

As such, they are primary drivers of the applications management agenda.

Process owners also receive direction for business process improvement from the users, and they drive and monitor user competency through the help desk and continuous education:

▶ Respond to enterprise program management (top) and user feedback (bottom)

▶ Cross lines of business, which can require process arbitration from the EPMO

▶ Drive the applications agenda

▶ Monitor and drive user competency through the help desk and continuous education

End users fulfill business processes, change the way they work to support improved business processes, provide feedback to process owners, and tap super users for support and the first level of problem resolution.

They receive fulfillment support from the help desk and receive relevant continuous training from user support:

▶ Fulfill business processes

▶ Provide feedback to process owners

▶ Tap the help desk for resolution

▶ Receive continuous training from user support

3.4.2 Enablement Domain

Super users train new end users and serve as "go-to" people who answer system functionality and business process questions. They also troubleshoot application problems and coach colleagues on the best practices for application deployment. One key purpose of this coaching is to increase user competence in regard to the role of fulfilling business processes and thus contributing to KPI improvement.

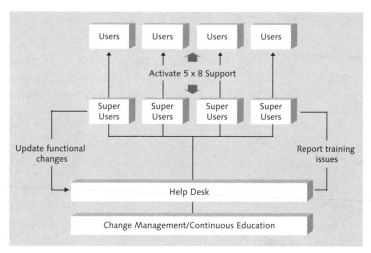

Figure 3.9 Enablement Domain: Defining End-User Training and Support

Super users also support configuration and programming teams to translate functional business requirements into technical requirements/specifications. Super users may assist in configuration unit and integration tests and usually fulfill user acceptance testing.

Organizational change management secures sponsorship of business process change across all stakeholder groups, develops and maintains an integrated change/risk management strategy and training program, and ensures that end users and business stakeholders are prepared to adopt new ways of work.

Continuous education groups develop integrated, role-based training specific to business process configuration. In support of this responsibility, they develop training channels and job aids to support new user roles, deliver initial training, and develop and deliver continuous training post-go-live, most pointedly when there are major business process changes, applications software upgrades or extensions, or both.

3.4.3 Applications Domain

Many firms do a fine job of creating and sustaining the enterprise and enablement domains. Where they often founder is in regard to the application domain due to either stubborn IT-centrism in regard to application configuration and maintenance or to a failure to secure direct business collaboration.

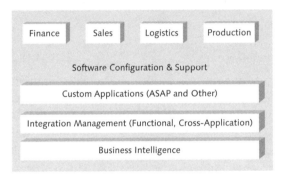

Figure 3.10 Applications Domain: Defining Applications Configuration, Development, and Functional Integration

The SAP configuration and support team, which resides within application management:

▶ Effects non-customized changes to applications software

▶ Provides custom application engineers with functional specifications both for interfacing requirements to legacy systems and for new custom applications that can't be engineered through enterprise software configuration

▶ Unit tests software changes

▶ Communicates process and system changes to the continuous education entity in the enablement domain.

This team may participate alongside super users in user acceptance testing.

Note that application management is not an IT-centric function. As such, staff assigned to SAP configuration will preferably come from the business community. For more about this, see Section 3.8 later in this chapter.

Integration management is responsible for cross-application integration testing and the handover to the IT support domain for technical integration, change management, and production control. This level of integration management is the nexus between a business-centric application management group and the IT support entity.

3.4.4 IT Support Domain

Business challenges come and go, but being shouted at in public tends to stick with you. Once, in the course of a presentation to about 40 people on this subject, I was interrupted by an attendee, who shouted, "You told us all this last year and we took your advice! We turned configuration over to our business staff and it was a mess! Complete chaos!"

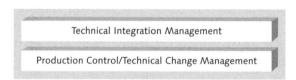

Figure 3.11 IT Support Domain: Defining Applications Support and Production Processes

In that one moment I was both flattered (the guy took my advice) and alarmed (he did use the word "chaos").

The reason for his anger and disappointment, it turned out, was that business people were also given the authority to promote configuration changes to production. Oops.

Once functional integration is complete, configurations must be turned over to IT. Technical integration is not a business-centric endeavor. This is the only "IT-centric" domain of the four, and it is responsible for integration management on a technical level, technical stress testing, promote-to-production, user authorities and security, and user and functional monitoring.

The IT domain is also on call for error handling and technical help desk (often via a vendor), as well as both production control and ongoing change management of applications software.

3.5 Transforming the "Build" Team into a Continuous Business Evolution Team

During enterprise application implementation projects, systems integrators join with client IT and business staff to form a project team primarily dedicated to business process design and subsequent configuring of software to fulfill that design. This team is usually complemented by other IT build teams that address reporting, interfacing, data migration, data warehousing, or custom applications.

Most clients erroneously dissolve these teams shortly after go live and revert to a traditional IT maintenance mode. This results in an incremental improvement rut and unnecessarily isolates IT from business. To ensure continuous business evolution, these teams should remain largely intact, with sufficient resources to not only maintain the initial to-be vision but also to drive evolution through extended applications, renewed business process improvement, and extended user competency.

During an implementation project, most of the Center of Excellence elements are already in working order. Process owners define business design with the applications management team, whose software changes are moved to integration management and subsequently production. Just prior to go-live, the remaining elements (namely help desk and the end-user population) are added. Help desk staff and end-user groups should be trained not only in the software being implemented, but also in the continuous business evolution methodology inherent in the Center of Excellence.

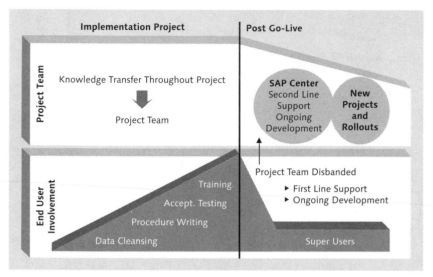

Figure 3.12 Transition from Project to Center of Excellence

In Figure 3.12, we can see that transitioning from an implementation organization to a Center of Excellence requires a planned draw-down (not the elimination) of the project team to a level capable of effective application management and support of business process change. By the same token, end users will shift from training mode to ongoing support mode, preferably one that is keynoted by a thriving super-user network.

3.6 Building a Center of Excellence

Presuming that you did not create a Center of Excellence in the course of your implementation, you will have to evolve into a Center of Excellence with a high level of enterprise authority and ongoing organizational change management.

Keys to success for such an undertaking include:

- **Clarity and authority**
  Successful completion of a charter that is agreed upon by a

firm's top executives. This charter is intended to provide a Center of Excellence with clarity and, most importantly, to establish the authority to make necessary organizational changes. Without such authority, the project will founder.

▶ **Successful branding**
A common understanding across the enterprise of how the Center of Excellence will be centered on measurable business results (preferably at the level of KPIs) and will thus be a driver of business improvement.

3.6.1   The Methodology

Our methodology, known as simply "The Bridge," because it spans from "the wedding/implementation" to "the marriage/long-term deployment" and includes three phases of activity:

1. **Initiation and assessment**
To establish high-level goals and the team composition and to measure the gaps between the current organization and the future organization.

2. **Justification and launch**
To establish the future organizational vision for developing a project charter for the building and deployment of a Center of Excellence that will be approved by senior management.

3. **Evolution planning**
To develop the master plan for changes to the organization, staffing, sourcing, budgeting, governance, and measurement.

As illustrated in Figure 3.13, the first two phases are linear, while the levels of activity for phase 3 may be overlapped to reduce the project duration.

Also illustrated in Figure 3.13, there is no end to the activity of evangelizing the identity and role of the Center of Excellence, just as there is no end to fulfilling the evolution plan. Continuity is the hallmark.

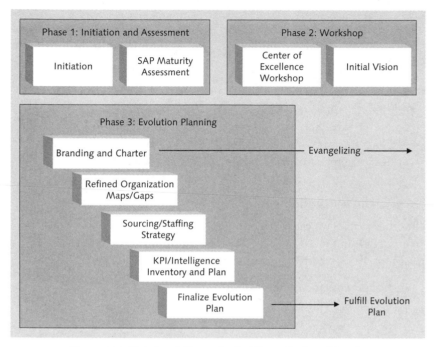

Figure 3.13 High-Level Phases for Building a Center of Excellence

In the detailed map in Figure 3.14, note that an early step is to assess your SAP maturity. Firms that do not take this step tend to take a much longer time to make organizational changes, on the faulty presumption that they already know what needs to be done. As a result, the gap analysis between their current state and envisioned state is incomplete.

Many Center of Excellence initiatives are immediately doomed to failure when firms leap immediately into evolution planning. Without knowledgeable grounding provided by initiation and assessment, and a justification that results in senior management approval, evolution will be hampered.

Further, if the charter for a Center of Excellence is centered on information technology, it is improbable that business stakeholders will embrace it.

	Phase	Level	Step	Name
Phase 1: Initiation & Assessment				
Level	1	1	0	Initiation
Step	1	1	1	Initiation Conference A
Step	1	1	2	Establish core team
Step	1	1	3	Establish base goals
Step	1	1	4	Initiation Conference B
Step	1	1	5	Update CoE workshop
Step	1	1	6	Draft initial CoE project charter
Level	1	2	0	SAP Maturity Assessment
Step	1	2	1	Establish respondents
Step	1	2	2	Survey
Step	1	2	3	Diagnostic and workshop update
Level	1	3	0	Center of Excellence Workshop
Step	1	3	1	Best practices presentation
Step	1	3	2	Review of assessment results
Phase 2: Justification				
Level	2	1	0	Initial Gap Analysis and Draft Plan
Step	2	1	1	Draft future organization
Step	2	1	2	Draft RACI
Step	2	1	3	Gap analysis (using assessment)
Step	2	1	4	High level transition plan
Level	2	2	0	Branding and Charter
Step	2	2	1	Name/brand center
Step	2	2	2	Create CoE charter
Step	2	2	3	Approve CoE charter
Step	2	2	4	Charter evangelization
Phase 3: Evolution Planning				
Level	3	1	0	Refine Organization Plan
Step	3	1	1	Refine organization map and gaps
Step	3	1	2	Refine RACI
Level	3	2	0	Sourcing/Staffing Strategy
Step	3	2	1	Identify internal staff
Step	3	2	2	Identify skills gaps
Step	3	2	3	Communications plan
Step	3	2	4	Determine sourcing method/partners
Step	3	2	5	Plan outsourcing
Level	3	3	0	Business Intelligence
Step	3	3	1	Inventory KPI requirements and hierarchy
Step	3	3	2	Business intelligence planning
Level	3	4	0	Finalize Evolution Plan
Step	3	4	1	Timeline and budget
Step	3	4	2	Outsourcing RFPs
Step	3	4	3	Staff reassignments
Step	3	4	4	Knowledge transfer master plan
Step	3	4	5	Run SAP review and knowledge transfer
Step	3	4	6	Senior approval of evolution plan

Figure 3.14 Detailed Steps for Building a Center of Excellence

The following are key milestones or deliverables for all phases:

1. Initial Center of Excellence project charter
2. Maturity assessment
3. Initial organization plan
4. Initial gap analysis
5. Initial transition plan
6. Center of Excellence charter
7. Master organization map
8. RACI (see end of Section 3.6.2)
9. Sourcing/staffing strategy
10. Business intelligence plan
11. Evolution plan

Phase 2 of this methodology includes the branding and charter for a Center of Excellence.

Poor branding is a reason often cited for a firm's failure to develop a Center of Excellence. The most frequent mistake is to include "SAP," "IT," or both in the name. Either of these sobriquets will ensure the scarcity of business people. The Center of Excellence should be named to attract, rather than repel, business membership. If an organization such as the one described herein is truly instituted, business people should be clamoring aboard, since business process owners, end users, and super users hold the power to determine how the enterprise functions.

3.6.2 Roles and Skillsets

Many career paths will be altered, and job transition will necessarily be a major undertaking. Table 3.2 shows the required skills for each role.

Function	Knowledge Required
Executives	
EPMO; Steering committee; C-level: funding, authority, and charter of the Center of Excellence	How they contribute to fulfillment of one or more business processes, where to go for help and/or more training, cross-functional software deployment
End Users	
System exploitation, training and re-training, exceptions reporting, user acceptance testing	How they contribute to fulfillment of one or more business processes, where to go for help and/or more training, cross-functional software deployment
Super Users	
5x8 support to end users, key contact for process rowners	Business process in the context of SAP, mastery of SAP functionality and tools, awareness of business intelligence sources, training skills
Help Desk	
Call center (frontend), functional assistance/referral	System navigation and connectivity troubleshooting, security tracing, typical application functional questions to query users when reporting problems
Process Owners	
Monitor business results, define business process improvements	Business/IT integration principle, process flow, SAP module basics, project methodology, business intelligence
Applications Management	
Software configuration to fulfill business process improvements, functional design for customizations, functional integration testing, user documentation of continuous end-user training	LOB business knowledge, business/IT integration principles, SAP configuration, business process flow, work flow, help desk procedures, project methodology
IT Support	
Production control/change management, middleware administration	Transport control, change management, hierarchy, instance management

Table 3.2 Functions and Required Skills

The following section contains thumbnail job descriptions for the most central roles in the Center of Excellence.

Executive Level/Steering Committee

▸ Fund, authorize, charter, and champion the Center of Excellence as the foundation for continually gaining value from the SAP and enterprise applications investments

▸ Provide direction to the EPMO with regard to company strategy and direction as a foundation for program management office budgets and priorities

▸ Where necessary, arbitrate cross-business issues arising from business process owners

Enterprise Program Management Office

▸ In the context of strategic direction from the executive level/steering committee, identify strategic cross-functional issues that SAP can enable (e.g., opportunities to gain efficiencies)

▸ Provide direction to the SAP business process leaders regarding business priorities and timelines

▸ Authorize budgets and monitor costs of application management, change management, and continuous training functions

▸ Arbitrate business process ownership issues

Business Process Owners

▸ Assess and monitor process performance and metrics with a focus on continuous process improvement

▸ Assess end-user input about process improvement

▸ Identify additional action items as needed to achieve continuous process improvement

▸ Maintain detailed knowledge of processes within assigned departments, and understand how processes transcend department boundaries and impact other functions within the organization

▶ Identify process/procedural changes to measurably improve overall process performance at a KPI level

▶ Work with business stakeholders to clarify and ensure linkage between system enhancements and business process benefits

▶ Work with other process owners and business leaders to assess cross-functional process metrics and performance

▶ In conjunction with the change management/continuous training group, regularly assess end-user competency and provide directives for raising the level

▶ Conduct feasibility studies for SAP system enhancements, evaluate system design, and determine cost/benefit and economic justification

▶ Review and evaluate the capabilities of existing systems for conformance to standards, and maintain a clear understanding of the system development and maintenance lifecycle

Super Users

A super user (or power user) is an end user who has in-depth knowledge and understanding of the SAP system and respective business processes utilizing SAP. This individual serves as a go-to person who can answer specific department-related system functionality and business process questions.

▶ Troubleshoot SAP-related problems and coach colleagues on using the system

▶ Support configuration specialists and help translate functional business requirements into technical requirements and specifications

▶ Communicate configuration/functionality changes to the business

▶ Participate in end-user acceptance testing

▶ Train new end users

- ▶ Keep knowledge of the system in a specific area of expertise up-to-date
- ▶ Contribute to the ongoing process development
- ▶ Report system problems/requests for enhancements to applications management

Application Management Leadership

Large organizations might have discrete leadership roles. Smaller organizations will have staff with combined application leadership and functional responsibilities.

Application leadership is the first-line contact for business process owners on one side and configuration support on the other. An application leader acts as project manager in terms of resource scheduling and assignments, budget/actual tracking, adherence to configuration and programming standards, and supervision of end-user acceptance testing and functional integration testing.

Application Management Staff

- ▶ Coordinate new SAP releases
- ▶ Oversee development and continued maintenance of SAP business process procedures, functional specifications, unit test scripts, integration test scripts and other associated documents
- ▶ Create SAP change requests and tasks using the Transport Organizer
- ▶ Enter configuration changes into the SAP development system
- ▶ Perform unit tests and integration tests of new and modified configurations
- ▶ Write functional specifications for new and changed interfaces
- ▶ Assist in unit and integration tests of new and changed interfaces with bolt-on software

- Assist in development and maintenance of training materials for departments

- Assist in performance and stress testing in conjunction with the Basis administration team

- Troubleshoot SAP configuration problems

- Coordinate changes to SAP based on OSS findings with the Basis team

- Determine training impact from new SAP releases (evaluate training delta requirements)

- Coordinate updated SAP business process procedures and related training documents to end users

- Coordinate continuing transports and refreshes for training clients (including Sandbox)

- Monitor configuration changes into the SAP Development System and determine impact on training materials and delta delivery (if required)

- Perform continual updates (as needed) to training tools (Knowledge Warehouse and On Demand, if applicable)

The combination of complete job descriptions with updated RACI charts provides each member of a Center of Excellence a solid understanding of their position, authorities, and relationships. These charts describe the order and content of key activities for each position in the Center of Excellence.

In the acronym RACI:

- **R** is for "responsible" and is the ultimate party responsible for all steps. This includes ultimate accountability that is limited to one individual.

- **A** is for "accountable," which means the designated party participates in the completion of the step and shares in its success or failure. More than one person may be accountable.

▸ **C** is "consulted." A consulted party is required to participate in the completion of a step but does not have the authority to reject that step.

▸ **I** is "informed." An informed party has no active role in the completion of a process step but needs to be aware of its content and completion.

There should be a RACI for every business process. Figure 3.15 shows an example.

		Business Process Owner	Business Stake-holder	Super User	End Users
1	Provide monitor roster	C	RA	C	I
2	Provide relevant material		RA	C	I
3	Schedule mentoring sessions		A	R	I
4	Complete mentoring session		I	R	A
5	Report mentoring results	I	A	R	C

R: Responsible **A:** Accountable **C:** Consulted **I:** Informed

Figure 3.15 Center of Excellence RACI

3.6.3 Direction and Duration

Each organization will have a different starting point and a different end vision; therefore, the effort required for each step will vary. Thus, this methodology provides a general direction, rather than a rigid and specific direction, and variations to individual steps in the methodology will occur.

3.6.4 A Note about Basis Administration

Savvy readers will have noted that we do not include Basis functions within the Center of Excellence. This not because we consider the functions to be trivial, but because they do not fit into the charter of a Center of Excellence (which focuses on business process excellence leading to measurable business benefit).

3.6.5 A Note about the Run SAP Methodology

In recent years, SAP unveiled the other side of the ASAP methodology known as Run SAP, which addresses continuous improvement to existing SAP installations. If your firm has installed SAP Solution Manager, Run SAP can be a useful methodology for your applications domain and can also benefit the enablement domain as well.

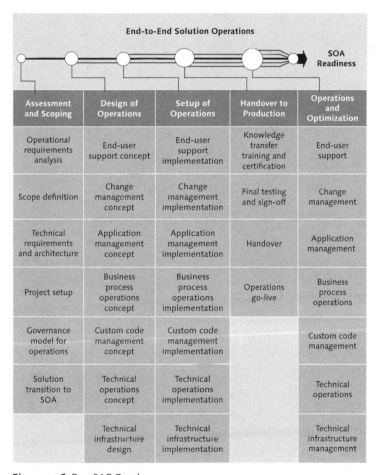

	End-to-End Solution Operations			SOA Readiness
Assessment and Scoping	**Design of Operations**	**Setup of Operations**	**Handover to Production**	**Operations and Optimization**
Operational requirements analysis	End-user support concept	End-user support implementation	Knowledge transfer training and certification	End-user support
Scope definition	Change management concept	Change management implementation	Final testing and sign-off	Change management
Technical requirements and architecture	Application management concept	Application management implementation	Handover	Application management
Project setup	Business process operations concept	Business process operations implementation	Operations go-live	Business process operations
Governance model for operations	Custom code management concept	Custom code management implementation		Custom code management
Solution transition to SOA	Technical operations concept	Technical operations implementation		Technical operations
	Technical infrastructure design	Technical infrastructure implementation		Technical infrastructure management

Figure 3.16 Run SAP Roadmap

As the map shown in Figure 3.16 illustrates, Run SAP conforms to the spirit of the Center of Excellence described here but does not embrace, to any great degree, the continuous business process improvement (with measurement) process, nor does it address business-centric planning.

3.7 Variant Structures for Centers of Excellence

The organizational structure of a Center of Excellence will vary depending on a client's application portfolio and site management.

Figure 3.17 shows a high-level example for a firm with one or more sites that have some functional or business process variations. In this example, there is still a centralized help desk, and the continuous education team provides support remotely.

In the remote locations, process oversight is relative to local process variations (e.g., orders to cash), and functional oversight is relative to local functional variations (e.g., methods for posting cash receipts).

The variant shown in Figure 3.18 addresses a smaller organization that does not require a formal EPMO. Line of business (LOB) leaders provide input and direction to a business process management entity charged with coordinating and integrating LOB business requirements and providing specifications, priorities, and requirements to a vendor governance group.

In this scenario, vendor governance manages two suppliers: an applications support group charged with providing user support and ongoing applications support and a hosting/support group charged with applications operations and Basis support.

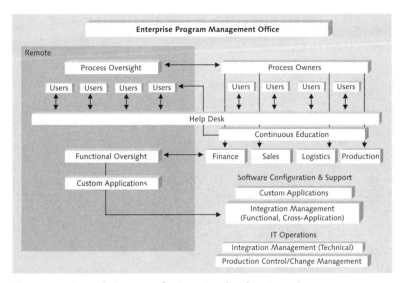

Figure 3.17 Example Structure for Functional and Business Process Variants

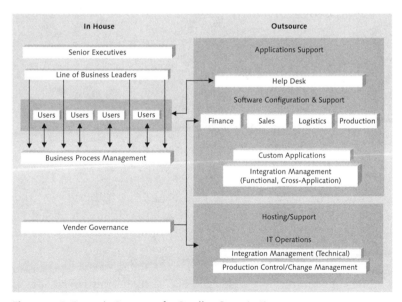

Figure 3.18 Example Structure for Smaller Organizations

3.8 Mastering the Business/IT Dynamic

Successful SAP lifecycle management is dependent on a healthy business and IT dynamic in which goals are aligned and with which IT supports are highly responsive to business change.

In this light, a new dynamic must replace the traditional organization between IT and business in which business personnel request IT services, define needs to IT representatives, and then await tested and implemented new or revised software.

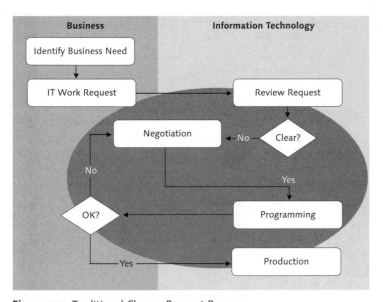

Figure 3.19 Traditional Change Request Process

In the traditional dynamic (see Figure 3.19), business makes requests to IT and is required to negotiate design and deadline. Negotiations and consequent programming/testing often have to be repeated, and this iterative loop is (a) extremely costly, (b) at the heart of business-IT antagonism, and (c) sloooow. Such a dynamic is nearly inevitable for legacy applications because they are program-based. If you run SAP and are still stuck in this dynamic, you have wasted a prime opportunity to evolve.

When both sides are collaborative, such a dynamic can function. However, let's be honest. This dynamic has been in place since the early 1960s. It consists of bargaining, negotiation, business people suspicious of IT terminology, and IT people suspicious of business needs. The result is often rancor. In short, this dynamic is at the heart of the failure to align business and IT.

The following are some common complaints:

▶ "I wanted a horse and got a cow."

▶ "The business people can't say clearly what they want or agree on their direction."

▶ "IT is too slow."

A more business-centric dynamic can be attained for enterprise applications because they are configuration-based, and much of the configuration can be accomplished by business staff.

A reminder:

▶ *Programming* is the creation of codes that direct the order, path, disposition, and destination of information.

▶ *Configuring* is the setting of business tables that direct the order, path, disposition, and destination of information.

While business-centric staff may not be positioned to complete all configuration, their leadership in this regard should eliminate the back and forth controls and negotiations that are central to the traditional change request process as illustrated in Figure 3.20.

Clearly, we do not leave it up business staff to complete the necessary IT testing (integration testing, stress testing, etc.) or to place configuration changes into production. All the same, we have vastly streamlined the process and made it fully business-centric.

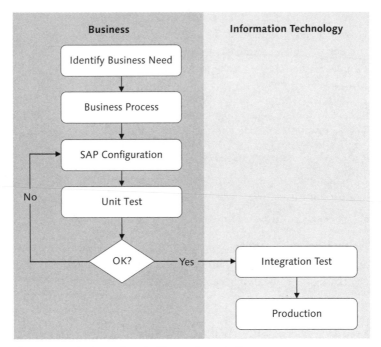

Figure 3.20 Business-Centric Change Request Process

3.9 A Word about SAP Solution Manager

SAP Solution Manager is the SAP-recommended tool for managing and sustaining your SAP applications. The focus of SAP Solution Manager is your SAP software platform, not your organization. In that light, a fully functional SAP Solution Manager is as beneficial to SAP as it is to you, in that SAP's maintenance is significantly simplified.

Mark Dendinger recommends deployment of this asset, saying that "Solution Manager can streamline a client's SAP performance management, thus liberating resources to concentrate on more strategic tasks."

The key benefits of SAP Solution Manager should be:

1. Enhanced visibility to SAP support (because while Solution Manager benefits clients, it also vastly reduces the burden of SAP support)
2. Enhanced visibility and control of SAP deployment (service-level reporting, diagnostics, change control, etc.)

If Solution Manager is deployed in the course of an implementation, seizing these benefits is a fairly straightforward endeavor. However, many clients and consultants have reported difficulties in retrofitting Solution Manager to an existing SAP installation. The steps required for this process are highly technical and thus do not fall under the charter of this book. Again, the Center of Excellence described in this chapter is focused on gaining vibrant business and IT alignment, which in turn gains measurable business benefit. All things considered, SAP Solution Manager can be an asset to your Center of Excellence.

3.10 When It All Goes Wrong: How Centers of Excellence Become Centers of Mediocrity

The following sections address common causes of Center of Excellence failure. While many firms succeed at building new organizations, these are the key reasons such organizations cannot be successfully sustained over time.

3.10.1 Leadership and Entropy

At about the time I got my start in the SAP world, I was heavily influenced by a wonderful book, *Management of the Absurd: Paradoxes in Leadership* by Richard Farson. In lively, witty, and elegant prose, Mr. Farson exposes a number of illusions about management and leadership and provides insight into why organizations fall into entropy. In my experience with SAP-installed base organizations, I have observed firsthand several these illusions and their deleterious effects.

Newly minted Centers of Excellence tend to sputter and disintegrate within mere months due to an over-reliance on leadership, vision, and nifty organization charts. A member of such an organization might say, "Joe was our leader. He was a great motivator and kept things together. Unfortunately, Joe's not here anymore, so we are back to the drawing board."

Resignations, reorganizations, mergers, and office politics can all lead to changes in your Center of Excellence, but the business world waits for no one. No entropy there. What holds a Center of Excellence together—what, in fact, makes a center excellent—is an organizational (all-hands) understanding of how business results direct your activities. Consider the example business situation below:

"Our customer satisfaction level was low (measure) due to slow delivery (measure). Our order fulfillment process was taking nine days (measure) so we streamlined the process down to six days (measure) and client satisfaction rose ten points (measure). Client complaints about our design process had nearly doubled (measure). We put our key clients on a portal for direct communication with our engineers. Pre-orders tripled (measure)."

In this example, we have a worry (low customer satisfaction) and have identified a cause (slow delivery). However, without measures of each, we have no idea if the worry is worth addressing or if the cause is actually the right one. Our solution has little to do with leadership and everything to do with facing and directly addressing a KPI (customer satisfaction). Here, business intelligence is the leader—not Joe. And business intelligence can always be available, whereas Joe may not be.

3.10.2   Business Process Orphanship

The notion of business process engineering was popularized in the mid-1990s by the bestseller *Reengineering the Corporation: A Manifesto for Business Revolution* by Michael Hammer and James Champy. However, it is difficult for many companies to shift an organizational mindset away from discrete vertical departments (marketing-sales-production-billing) into fully operational and horizontal business process units. Therefore, the role of business process ownership is only partially baked into the business conscience, and fulfilling that role can be perilous.

Since most business processes cross departmental boundaries, their "owners" are often at odds with department heads with turf issues. Without a clear charter and authority from on high, a business process owner is constantly buffeted by resistance to process change. The result is an inability to improve business processes beyond the tinkering stage, which does not result in any appreciable business benefit. In such a situation, business process ownership is business process orphanship.

Back when I was first researching best practices for post-implementation SAP solutions, I had the good fortune to work with Jack Childs of SAP America, whose task was supporting the major North American SAP accounts and whose insight into client efforts was invaluable. In 2003, Mr. Childs administered an informal poll regarding the role of a business process owner and found that the shelf life was only two years. Reasons for this short shelf life were unsurprising: high stress, low authority, inability to succeed.

Brian Dahill's field experience tells him that too many companies resist changing their ways. "They feel that best practices don't apply to them because they are too different from other companies. In essence, they suffer from their misplaced sense of uniqueness."

If you do not invest good business process owners with proper executive support, you should not bother building a Center of Excellence. Of all the roles included, it is the most vital.

3.10.3 Super Users Cast Adrift

Many years ago, I was on a long call with a Gateway technician who was helping me save my hard drive. While various operations were running, she regaled me with stories, both her own and some recounted by others, of strange help desk calls. The client whose foot-pedal didn't work. It was the mouse. The client whose cup holder was broken. The CD tray. The client who only got a black screen. The video wasn't plugged in. And finally, everyone's favorite: the client who could not find the "Any" key to save his life.

The hour I spent with the Gateway technician cost my company nothing; nor were the aforementioned callers charged for their queries because none of us were using an in-house help desk. For those of you with one of these, we have to ask the question How much of your time is spent explaining that a mouse is not a foot pedal and a CD tray is not a cup holder?

On many occasions, I have had the fascinating task of assessing a client's SAP help desk statistics. Call volume, average call time, average resolution time, and the like are invariably categorized as such, but I have yet to see the category "mindless waste of time," so I have no statistical handle on the frequency of such calls in an SAP environment.

However, there has been one simple trend to every help desk analysis I have ever been a part of, and that is the very high percentage of calls that relate to "end-user training"—that is, calls that would not be necessary if end users were properly trained and supported.

According to a 2008 study by Insite Objects, Inc., 72% of firms with SAP have some form of super-user organization. Our observation is that the life span and utility of super users varies from place to place. The importance of super users cannot be understated. When properly motivated and deployed, they raise end-user competency and, consequently, the business benefit of SAP deployment.

The proper ratio of super users to end users is 1 to 10 or 20. Super users should be available for one-on-one coaching, group update training, and some level of analysis regarding what might be done to improve overall end-user competency.

The super-user function is not full-time, and managers often feel that employee time given over to this function is lost. The pressures on super users include (a) demanding front-line jobs that leave inadequate time to fulfill the super user role, (b) lack of management support, (c) inadequate documentation or tools for ongoing SAP training, and (d) faulty or over-specialized business processes that render SAP functions too clunky and hard to promote. When these pressures come to bear, super users drop their gloves and stick close to their front-line jobs.

Without such enablement support, individual end users don't keep up their SAP skills, don't extend their SAP skills, and feel burdened by changes to processes or functions.

A few of my former colleagues have long labored selling SAP end-user training courses. The value of their courses is huge, but that value is chronically rejected. Years ago, in a study of 120 firms in the installed base, I asked two questions:

1. Who in your firm is responsible for SAP end-user competency?
2. Who in your firm controls the budget for SAP end-user training?

When responses were expressed in bar charts, the bars for "Don't know" and "No one" towered over the others (IT director, HR director, VP of ERP, CIO, et al.), something like in Figure 3.21.

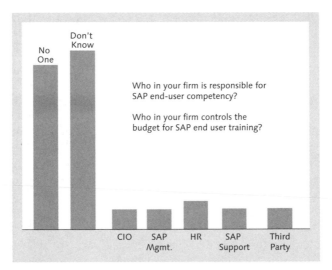

Figure 3.21 Clients Lacking Ownership for SAP Competency

A help desk is a great start toward resolving this issue. Consider the help desk AAA, and super users a GPS system. Lost or misdirected users cost money and fail to effectively fulfill business processes. This is precisely how your SAP return-on-investment goes right out the side door while you are gazing at the ceiling.

3.10.4 Burial by SAP

Most of us have known people who have classic cars in their garages that they never drive. Instead, they are constantly tinkering with the engine or shining the hood or polishing the glass. Some SAP IT shops are like that as their leadership buys into more SAP offerings than can be efficiently absorbed, usually at the cost of business focus. In past years, SAP has presented various initiatives relative to SAP Competency Center, SAP Customer Care Center, and the like, and in every case the key subject was more efficient deployment of SAP software. While SAP has advanced many miles in the right direction, never forget that SAP software performance (the engine) is but a subset of the larger and more cogent subject: business results.

As seen in this chapter, there are many moving parts to a successful Center of Excellence, and all of them involve people. You may be thinking that everyone you need will be internally identified, but that should not necessarily be the case. The alternative— intelligent sourcing—is fully explored in the next chapter, We Do It Themselves: Outsourcing SAP Applications Support.

Too many clients seek to "do it all themselves." This is nei-ther wise nor cost effective. This chapter enlightens clients to the judicious use of external and remote services.

4   We Do It Themselves: Outsourcing SAP Applications Support

Distinguishing strategic work from non-strategic work is a challenge for many SAP clients. The following chapter elaborates how outsourcing of non-strategic work can help clients focus on their strategic challenges: in other words, moving beyond a simplistic yes or no outsourcing proposition.

4.1   We Do It Themselves

The notion of accomplishing in-house everything under the IT sun arose in the 1970s with the advent of what were then called mini-computers, prominently supplied by firms such as Digital Equipment and Data General. (I started my career in 1974 on Digital Equipment's PDP-11.) Prior to the availability of mini-computers, firms that could not afford mainframes worked on a time-share basis; they were, in essence, outsourcing their hosting, disaster recovery, and infrastructure maintenance. During this same period, vendors finally decoupled hardware and software (that's right, you used to have to buy them in a bundle). This decoupling gave rise to software houses to which software development was...outsourced.

One comment that has been repeated to me by clients over the years in regard to IT projects is "We're in the [fill in the blank] business, not the IT business." They are expressing their desire to return to core business activities and get out from under the details of information technology maintenance.

An extremely bright Basis specialist I know recently told me that IT directors will not outsource because they are fearful of giving up even a portion of the full-time equivalents who report to them. Clearly, this may be a valid fear in many cases, but such an attitude has more to do with turf protection than with driving value for a firm. As for the consequential argument of "But I can't control outside staff," I would counter with "What do you prefer—controlling a number of individual employees or one or two vendor contacts?" At any rate, it is outcomes you should be managing, not people.

The final decision fulcrum remains: How far do you want to extend yourself with activities that are not strategic? And what business momentum could you provide your firm with the time that delegating frees up?

4.2 Applications Are What We Do

Early in the new millennium, several clients asked me which service providers could help them to plan and build a Center of Excellence. To get a handle on these requests, I contacted SAP leaders at all of the usual suspects (Accenture, Deloitte, IBM, BearingPoint, and CapGemini) as well as several second-tier firms. All initially assured me that they provided such a service, but all hedged dramatically when pressed for a methodology, references, and costing. Instead, I was invariably ushered into a meeting with the head of a nascent applications outsourcing practice in which I was assured that applications outsourcing was the wave of the future.

Thwarted in my attempt to find firms that could build SAP Centers of Excellence, I turned my attention back to clients to see how interested they'd be in outsourcing their applications.

During a presentation to a group of META Group clients in Chicago about post-implementation SAP strategies, I was asked again if service providers had a methodology and service offering for helping build them. No, I replied, but they would offer to take over the applications in an outsourcing environment. To gauge audience interest, I asked for a show of hands of those who would consider outsourcing the management of their SAP applications. No hands were raised, but many voices were heard. Whatever SAP accreditation I had earned to that point in the presentation was largely lost, as both my wisdom and sanity were questioned. I especially remember a VP of IT laughing loudly and remarking, "Applications are what we do."

About a year later, we did some primary research that indicated that 41% of respondents would not even consider outsourcing the management of their applications. This part of our research was a standard "adoption scale" in which respondents told us in what time frame they might consider adopting a given technology or service. We had never seen such a high percentage of "will not consider" responses.

While resistance is still extant, service providers continue to offer application outsourcing, which is called by various names: application maintenance outsourcing (AMO), application management outsourcing (also AMO), or application management services (AMS). (Yes, another confusing set of three-letter acronyms.) The letter that bothers potential clients the most is that big M, as in "management." It would help immeasurably if the vendors simply offered support.

In more recent years, client acceptance of the service has risen as the notion of "Applications are what we do" has morphed into "Why are we maintaining these applications ourselves?"

Service provider quality remains mixed, primarily because too many of the service providers have poor or unproven delivery models. More on this to follow.

If you have not considered outsourcing your applications, this chapter should challenge you to do so. If you are already considering outsourcing your applications, this chapter should provide you a roadmap.

For the sake of clarity, I will be addressing two levels of application outsourcing:

► **Application maintenance**
Keeping the lights on—basic applications hosting/operations, break/fix, de-bug, backup, etc.

► **Application management**
Providing more light—maintenance functions (above) plus a level of application improvement, upgrade, and/or business process transformation

For the latter, there are various levels of management:

► Functional application enhancement as needed to assure basic continuity

► Frequent application enhancements to provide some optimization

► Defined levels/stages of business process transformation

The difference between optimization and transformation is enormous. In optimization mode, you are improving the as-is state of your applications. In transformation, you are moving to another to-be state. If optimization is like tuning your car, then transformation is like getting a whole new car.

When people say "Applications are what we do," they are thinking more about optimization and transformation than about continuity. In this regard, a key misconception regarding the outsourcing of applications support is that clients are relinquishing control of management when in fact they may only be giving up redundant, low-level, non-strategic labor and still keeping both hands on the applications steering wheel. There is still a capital W to the "We do it themselves" concept.

4.3 Why on Earth Would We Outsource Our Applications?

The key value statements a plethora of application outsourcers offer usually center on (a) economy and (b) superior SAP skills.

Whatever the veracity of these statements, it is probable that you are looking for something else. Perhaps the cost of maintaining your SAP applications is acceptable but not predictable, due to occasional spikes in demand. Perhaps your internal SAP staff is competent, but you are chronically short of some key skills.

Table 4.1 shows some of the key advantages and disadvantages to SAP application outsourcing.

Outsourced Application Management		Client Staff (In-House)	
Advantage	Disadvantage	Advantage	Disadvantage
Steeped in method and consulting skills	No direct stake in operational success (unless contractually)	Direct stake in operational success	Less knowledge of method and consulting skills
Costs may be shared across multiple clients on an as-needed or as-used basis.	May lack single client focus.	Single client focus is assured.	Costs are not flexed according to usage.
Deeper product experience			Shallow product experience
	Not deeply oriented to client business context and organization	Fully oriented to client business context and organization	

Table 4.1 Outsourcing vs. Managing Applications In-House

Outsourced Application Management		Client Staff (In-House)	
Advantage	Disadvantage	Advantage	Disadvantage
Better exposure to industry best practices	May not have the capacity/skills to manage a mix of enterprise and legacy applications.	Greater experience with legacy applications	Less exposure to industry best practices
Deeper knowledge of business process design			Shallow knowledge of business process design

Table 4.1 Outsourcing vs. Managing Applications In-House (Cont.)

If your in-house staff is chronically weak at methodology and people skills, outside resources may be a boon. As for a direct stake in operational success, your in-house people have face time that an outside provider will not, though with good governance, you can be sure that your provider will have a stake in your success.

One major advantage to outsourcing applications, especially in an on-demand environment, is the economy of resource coupled with predictability of service. Many firms assign in-house SAP staff to support roles and project roles on a 50-50 basis, only to find that a type of scenario occurs as in Figure 4.1.

Applications support is a little bit like the emergency room, and SAP installations have their "full moons," so the predictability of support demand is compromised, as is staff availability for projects.

In Figure 4.1 we see a situation in which half of a firm's SAP FTEs are allocated to support and the other half to projects. For both sides, there will be spikes or lags in demand. While the business impact on support will be up and down, the business impact for projects is much more dramatic. Adding even a modest amount of outside staff for "spikes" will largely eliminate these shocks.

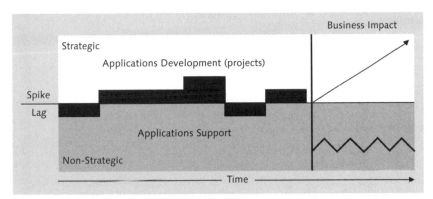

Figure 4.1 Applications Support Demand Is Highly Variable

On the subject of product experience (relative to SAP), service providers do not always have more depth. A client of mine once complained that a potential provider claimed five-plus years of SAP experience on average. "We've had SAP for ten years," my client told me, "and most of my staff is still with me."

If your SAP applications are heavily customized or heavily interfaced with other applications (or both), this uniqueness will hamper your ability to outsource more than one or two support levels.

If you are contracting for applications management, business process skills come into play. While in-house staff knows your business process better than outsiders, the outsiders will normally have greater knowledge of the best business processes due to greater client exposure. Outsiders may also have better insight about how to link business performance metrics to business processes.

From direct experience and through primary research, these three reasons are most often cited for outsourcing SAP applications support:

1. Bridge a skills or expertise gap
2. Provide a more predictable cost and business response
3. Free up staff from banal maintenance to concentrate on more strategic issues

Reasons 1 and 2 are fairly obvious. Reason 3 goes deeper than it looks.

After the first great wave of SAP implementations arrived on the post-Y2K shore, there was a glut of underemployed SAP consultants across the United States. Many found refuge by returning to industry in a maintenance role. For most of these people, boredom quickly set in. Without the adrenalin of project-based work—the challenges, the deadlines, the pressing need to constantly upgrade their skills—they found themselves turning into clock-watchers and could not wait to head back out into the field once the market picked up.

There are similar effects for in-house staff if the day-to-day work concentrates on (a) maintaining interfaces, (b) de-bugging, and (c) responding to user queries. What we see is a split of duties between exciting new stuff (a small percentage) and boring daily maintenance (a large percentage). While the notion of "Applications are what we do" has its merits, I think what we mean is closer to "Improving and expanding applications is what we want to do." Without "at-hand" outside help, the as-is has a persistent way of trumping the to-be.

Figure 4.2 is a simplified schematic of heavily outsourced SAP support.

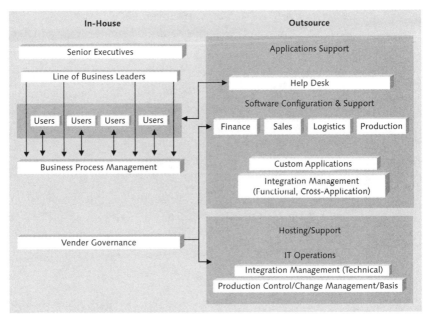

Figure 4.2 Scenario for Outsourced SAP Support

4.4 Application Outsourcing Adoption

In this section, we will explore ways to assess your organizational readiness to outsource your applications to some level (either maintenance or management). While such an assessment might ultimately point to your *lack* of readiness, it should also provide a diagnostic for how you can get ready.

Table 4.2 is an adoption model from your internal organizational alignment to execution of the service. For each of the five stages of adoption, there are four key focus categories:

1. **State of applications**
   How reasonable is it to presume that outsiders can maintain your applications? If they are extremely unique (that is, highly customized or heavily interfaced) or in disarray, then handover will be compromised.

2. **Environment/risk/change management**
   Careful targeting of the applications to be outsourced and how that outsourcing should occur are at the heart of outsourcing success. Particular attention should be given to planning forward governance of the to-be-chosen vendor.

3. **End users and supports**
   The key constituents of outsourced application maintenance are the users, so we highly recommend preparing them and including them in outsource planning.

4. **Skills**
   This category of activity is a combination of (a) assessing what skills must be retained in-house for strategic activities and what skills are needed from an outsourcing vendor, and (b) preparing individuals to effectively perform vendor governance.

Level		State of Applications	Environment/ Change Management	End-Users and Support	Skills
1	Aligned	Applications to be outsourced are fully implemented and required interfacing is complete.	Determination of specific applications under consideration and applications not to be.	End-users and super-users are identified.	Identification of specific skills sets associated with applications is complete.
2	Assessed	Have acceptable levels of a) customization and b) quality, nature, and volume of interfacing.	Goals and objectives of application outsourcing are established and measured.	Help desk traffic and end user competency have been assessed.	Determination of cost of skills associated with specific application(s) (e.g., prof. development, training, retention, and recruiting).

Table 4.2 SAP Application Outsourcing Adoption Model

Level	State of Applications	Environment/ Change Management	End-Users and Support	Skills
3 **Planned**	Final determination of the level of outsourcing to be contracted has been agreed.	Vendor governance relative to business process change (and consequent change management) is in place.	Super user input regarding planned services has been provided.	Identification and selection of potential governance team has been made.
4 **Selected**	Blueprint of applications management roles and processes is complete.	Outsourcing staff are vetted, contract and due diligence are complete, and transition plan is in place.	Super users agree with vendor selection and transition plan.	Governance team and transitioning staff have met with chosen provider.
5 **Executed**	Application migration to service provider commences, provider assumes responsibility for application deployment, availability and management.	Contract signed, transition plan begins, risk mitigation processes exercised, employee transition occurs.	Application support requests are successfully routed, logged, and addressed.	Transition, retention, outplacement, and retooling are complete.

Table 4.2 SAP Application Outsourcing Adoption Model (Cont.)

Though the five levels of adoption (alignment, assessment, planning, selection, and execution) do not have to be completed sequentially, an agreed-upon point of closure for each level should be met.

In detail, these levels consist of:

▶ **Alignment**

Clients attain this level only if the key constituents (business stakeholders, SAP support team, and user community) are on the same page. Firms need to address reasons they should consider outsourcing, candidate functions or areas to be outsourced, and the desired results to be achieved through outsourcing. High-level business case formulation, risk assessment, and goal formulation are at the core of this level.

▶ **Assessment**

Completion of this level is categorized through base case assessment of capabilities and functions in consideration for outsourcing. These assessments examine current base costs and projected future costs of providing these services internally. Factors to consider include uniqueness of the function to the business (current and projected), skills retention and development (current and projected), and comparison (benchmark) to current market offerings.

▶ **Planning**

The planning phase begins with the selection of specific functions to outsource and continues through business case development, risk assessment and mitigation planning, service provider identification, and bid process development. Expectations are level-set regarding original intentions and objectives for outsourcing. Internal sourcing and governance teams are established.

▶ **Selection**

This level is completed when the vendor selection is completed. The sourcing team has reviewed competitive bids by comparing the base case and scenario planning conducted in the assessment and planning phases, vendors have completed due diligence surrounding the function to be outsourced, and the client has received a best and final offer. Vendors are evaluated on competitiveness (to each other and market prices established during the assessment phase), responsiveness, manageability, and adaptability.

▶ **Execution**
This phase is characterized by the establishment and implementation of governance policies, procedures, processes, and controls as part of contractual execution (formal conclusion of the deal). To satisfactorily complete this level, a client should establish an initial service level agreement (and language affording modification), definition of services to be provided (including line-item pricing), benchmarking clauses and time lines, change, problem, incident, and escalation management procedures.

What you do not want to do is make the same mistake as a depressingly high percentage of clients: Make it up as you go. Even worse is simply deciding to outsource and immediately searching for a provider. Following a reasonable adoption model might lead you to conclude that it is not feasible or desirable to outsource your applications support. Following a random adoption model will certainly lead to future problems managing your provider or lead you to drop the idea altogether, whatever its merits.

4.5 Crossing the Bridge from Maintenance to Management

Many clients are far more comfortable outsourcing the maintenance of applications rather than the management.

In a maintenance environment, the client still holds the baton and chooses the sheet music while a service provider takes care of the orchestra members.

In a management environment, the client still holds the baton, but a service provider writes the requested tunes and provides the sheet music to the orchestra. In essence, the client maintains control over what is to be done to applications but cedes control in terms of how.

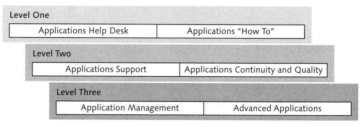

Figure 4.3 Levels of Applications Support

Various providers offer varying levels of support, and they tend to break down as follows (see Figure 4.3; contents are partial and vary from vendor to vendor):

▶ **Level 1: Applications help desk**

  ▶ Respond to end-user and super-user queries about features and functions (an applications "how to")

  ▶ Maintain end-user documentation

  ▶ Report and run diagnostics for level 2 and 3 applications support staff

▶ **Level 2: Applications support**

  ▶ De-bug and patch defective applications via configuration or customization

  ▶ Test and apply SAP updates and patches relative to applications

  ▶ Extend remote end-user training

  ▶ Perform upgrade support (testing, loading, and production of SAP upgrade version)

▶ **Level 3: Applications management**

  ▶ Perform custom reporting via ABAP or the relevant SAP tool (SAPscript, business intelligence, etc.)

▶ Perform SAP application systems extensions via configuration, customization, or both (extension or improvement of existing application, new application, SAP-approved bolt-on)

▶ Oversee interfacing between SAP and legacy/other applications

▶ Implement end-user training relative to application extension or improvement

▶ Oversee knowledge transfer to client SAP support team relative to extension or improvement

▶ Update user and technical documentation relative to extension or improvement

▶ Extend upgrade support (strategy, blueprinting, configuration, testing, production)

▶ Perform audit compliance support (often included in level 2)

In many cases, application management can simply be handled through a combination of help desk and periodic staff augmentation services.

Some vendors actually suggest that you even give up the baton and just let them run the applications in toto. Such an arrangement leaves the client fully dependent on the vendor, which strikes me as the sinker that follows hook and line.

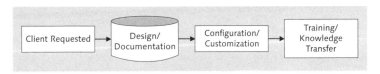

Figure 4.4 Linear and Simplified Issue Resolution

Further, returning to the theme of "Applications are what we do," take a look at the list of applications management tasks and consider which, if any, are in the wheelhouse of strategic activities.

Moving directly from full in-house applications support to full-blown applications management may not be a wise move. A popular alternative is the big toe approach by which clients start out with application maintenance (help desk for users, issues management, and some report writing) and gradually extend the outsourcing footprint. Following the SAP Application Outsourcing Adoption Model, you can best decide to what level you should begin outsourcing during the alignment and assessment steps.

Local and Remote Delivery Models

I am using the term "local" loosely here. Only in rare instances does your outsourcing vendor actually place its delivery staff in your location. In this context, think of local as within your cultural and geographic domain despite the fact that the services provided come from a remote location, even when that location is across the street.

Level 1 (help desk) is straightforward. An authorized end user calls a help number or enters an issue into a help desk website. The issue is acknowledged, classified, prioritized, and resolved (usually in less than an hour and often during the course of an initial phone call).

More complex issues will be routed directly to level 2 (technical support) for resolution. Level 2 issues usually take from one to eight business hours for resolution.

Any term that creates more confusion than clarity should be scrapped. This applies to the term "offshore." As it happens, this expression is only used in North America. Elsewhere, the realm of services that can be supplied from any remote location is known as "global sourcing." But even this term can be misleading. If you are located in Boston and your SAP applications support provider is in South Dakota, it is certainly not offshore and very probably not global.

I therefore settle on the term "remote" for services that are provided from outside your cultural or geographic boundaries.

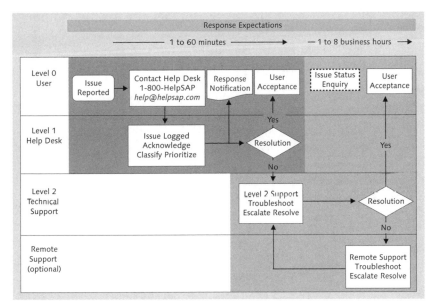

Figure 4.5 SAP Help Desk Process

In *The New SAP Blue Book: A Concise Business Guide to the World of SAP*, I describe a local/remote combination of delivery resource for new implementations that can be very beneficial. While a mix of local and remote resources for SAP support can also be beneficial, a different set of considerations applies. The most important of these revolves around a continuous need for effective communication. In an implementation setting, end users are not contacting remote sites for assistance, and it is the initial end user/help desk relationship that is at the heart of successful SAP outsourced support.

Note that in Figure 4.5, a level 2 issue can be consigned to a remote support site for resolution. Suppliers that provide both local and remote support are able to (a) directly address a client in a comfortable cultural and geographic setting (same language, time zone, etc.) and (b) where needed, tap into a deeper and more diverse remote talent pool that will also cost less than the local resource. (Rates vary from country to country and firm to firm, but a thumbnail comparison is that a qualified U.S.-based applications support consultant will cost from $120 to $160 per hour, or at least twice the rate of a qualified "remote" applications support consultant.)

When people talk or write about "cheap offshore resources," they usually fail to comprehend that the deployment of this resource varies considerably. It is one thing to email specifications from Boston to Shanghai for Java programming, and quite another to perform business process design between a Boston client and a Shanghai consultant.

When using a local/remote supplier for SAP applications support, a client should insist on the deployment of a proven web-based communications platform (see Figure 4.6). Emails and phone calls should be kept to a minimum. "Visibility" is the key word here, as a client should be able to see the following at any time:

1. Pending issues (by type, priority, and point of origin)

2. Scheduling (resource, estimated resolution time)

3. Closed and resolved issues log

4. Rolling costs

5. Document repository (includes general documents and is indexed by issue)

This is the information a client needs in any case, whether the help desk resource is on Mars or one floor up.

In addition to a robust communications platform, an SAP applications support supplier should also provide rich statistics that will drive a diagnostic from help desk activity. As elaborated later, I have long observed that a very high percentage of help desk tickets relate to training issues.

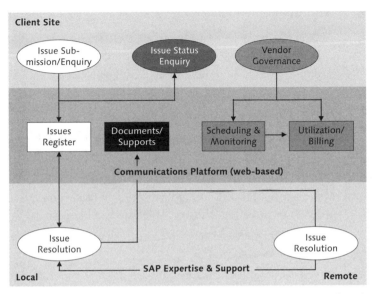

Figure 4.6 A Communications Platform for Connecting Client, Local, and Remote Support

4.6 Governance for Outsourced SAP Applications Support

Failure to manage your vendor will quickly and directly lead to project failure. This is not because the service providers will take advantage of you (though they might) but because, without your governance, the service providers will not be positioned to succeed for you. Two ugly phrases that persist in this marketplace are "vendor: your mess for less" and "client: we can throw all this over the wall."

Unless yours is a fairly small organization, you will necessarily have more than one person involved in vendor governance. These are the four key subject areas of vendor governance:

- ▶ **Relationship governance: daily**
  - ▶ Executive steering: keeping the vendor aware of current priorities or business issues
  - ▶ Problem resolution: following end-user satisfaction
  - ▶ Service request process: ensuring that communication between users and vendor support is functional
  - ▶ Escalation process: supervising or monitoring exceptional issues
- ▶ **Performance processes: weekly**
  - ▶ Service-level tracking and reporting: A credible vendor will provide credible reporting on at least a weekly basis.
  - ▶ Service-level review: Vendor reports should be validated with the user community.
  - ▶ Benchmarking: Performance thresholds can be modified to spur improvement (see the upcoming section about fee strategies).
- ▶ **Contract processes: quarterly or biannual**
  - ▶ Negotiation management
  - ▶ Contract management
  - ▶ Contractor management
  - ▶ Scope change process
- ▶ **Technical processes: as needed**
  - ▶ Production acceptance and change management: This applies to configuration changes and thus to an application management scenario.
  - ▶ Governance compliance
  - ▶ Architectural compliance

All of the above speak to governance, but it really comes down to governing, by which I mean that having the structure and the necessary paperwork will give you a framework, but actually performing the governance is what matters most.

If your firm is also outsourcing hosting or Basis administration (or both), then your governance on the technical end may be multi-vendor. This will require a second level of governance focusing on the vendor-to-vendor relationship. This does not have to be as complex as the relationship between application management and technical teams, as described in Chapter 3, Building and Sustaining a Center of Excellence.

4.7 Fee Strategies

While there are a variety of fee models for application support, the majority are a fixed fee with a time and materials rate for overage:

▸ A standard fixed fee for a packet of pre-determined hours

▸ A standard hourly fee for time in excess of the base amount

The obvious weakness of such an arrangement is that clients may get stuck paying for unused time but will always have to pay when that base time is exceeded.

The way around this is to arrange a fixed fee that takes into account three- to six-month averages rather than simply month to month. Thus, if a vendor spends less than the allotted time in some months and more in others, costs will balance out to the client's benefit.

In essence, what you get with a fixed fee is some predictability of cost, but that's it. Service providers working for a fixed fee have little financial motivation to do anything more than deliver the prescribed services. This is a subject where I often start afresh with service providers, especially when they claim a desire to be "partners" with their clients.

To promote partnership status, clients should consider fee models to the right of the fixed fee in Figure 4.7.

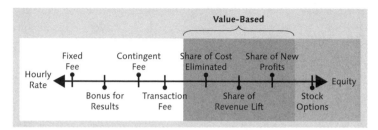

Figure 4.7 Fee Models for Application Support

Paying a bonus for good results (e.g., a high percent of call resolutions in a short window of time) will provide the vendor with motivation, but such an arrangement should be counterbalanced by getting a credit back for bad results (e.g., low percent of call resolutions or long timeframes).

Some clients have exhibited a preference for paying a transaction fee, a more on-demand approach by which each help desk ticket is billed individually by time spent. The unpredictable nature of client demand in this regard leads providers to charge higher hourly rates than for a fixed-fee arrangement.

Gain-sharing methods lead to the highest level of client-vendor partnerships since providers are motivated to help clients reduce costs and raise revenues. The downside of such arrangements is that measurement is required. This is an area in which most clients are weak.

Further, gain-sharing fee models lend themselves primarily to application management and strategic efforts, as opposed to application maintenance and keeping-the-lights-on tasks.

The simplest method to govern is a fixed fee with some sort of risk/reward kicker based on support results in which the initial bar is set at whatever support levels were provided in-house (before transition to the provider). Clients seeking to continually raise this bar should remember that there are, quite naturally, diminishing opportunities to improve. For example, if an initial benchmark for closing out help desk issues is 95% and a service provider improves that figure to 98%, the benchmark should not be going up.

If you are seeking cost reductions, the local/remote model as explained in Section 4.5 can be very attractive, provided that there are (a) sufficient local resources for language and cultural comfort and (b) a solid web-based communications platform.

One final note about fee strategies: You should be getting some form of concession based on the length of contract. While this may seem obvious, it is not always the case in the real world. An important negotiating point for new adopters is that if you start out with a one-year contract, you should include wording to the effect that an extension, prior to completion of the first year, will result in, at minimum, no raise in fees for the extension period. The point of this is that after the first year, a client could become a captive audience and thus be vulnerable to price hikes for years two, three, and beyond.

4.8 Basis Is Eternal (and Can Be Done from Anywhere)

Throughout the lifecycle of SAP business applications, Basis support is a necessity.

Not everyone is fully aware of what Basis is or what Basis people do. Consider this definition of Basis from *searchSAP.com*: "Basis is a set of middleware programs and tools…provides the underlying base (thus the name) that enables applications (such as FI, CO, and SD, for example) to be interoperable and portable across operating systems and database products."

What Basis people do on a regular, um, basis:

▶ Daily monitoring of system performance

▶ Database administration

▶ Operating system administration

What Basis people do as needed:

▶ Upgrades

▶ User administration

▶ Support packages

▶ Hardware migrations

As previously noted, Basis support is not necessarily an integral part of the Center of Excellence because it does not directly address business process fulfillment and evolution. However, without solid Basis support, you might experience unnecessarily long response times, database anomalies, and overly complex upgrades, all of which will degrade business process fulfillment and the nervous systems of most end users.

Basis work is techie stuff, which tends to give rise to the terms "Basis Geek," "Basis Wonk," "Techno-Weenie," or worse. As it happens, the relative value of a Basis specialist can vary; that variation is often a matter of whether or not an individual is keeping up with the technology.

I am reminded of an internal debate some years ago at META Group about the offshore outsourcing of programming jobs. While one side of the debate argued that America was losing its technical talent, my colleague Stan Lepeak questioned whether the country is losing highly talented software engineers or video gaming "Java jockeys."

The softer point to be made here is that it is unwise to simply grab a "Basis Geek" or two and consider the matter settled. The variation of needs must be matched by a variation of skills, some of which may be required in-house on a full-time basis, and others that may best be outsourced.

4.8.1 Delivery from Anywhere

Vendor distance matters when you're ordering a pizza. It matters much less for Basis support. As in, not at all.

During implementation, project managers love to have a Basis person at hand even when that person is not fully occupied because when they are needed, that need is urgent. This urgency is noted by clients who tend to ask how many Basis people they will need on-site after go-live. My classic consultant response in years past was "It depends," but in recent years my response has been "Very likely zero."

After go-live there are fewer urgencies relative to daily Basis administration. Outside of organizations with more than $1 billion in annual revenues or with very large user populations, few firms really need full-time in-house Basis staff unless they are continually in roll-out mode, continually tinkering with software add-ons, or did a very poor job of implementing. I regularly receive requests from clients for "a temporary Basis guy"; the scope of requirements for such requests is a smorgasbord of upgrade assistance, enhancement pack, support for a business intelligence project, and, oh yes, we'd also like some ABAP programming support. In past years, my response was to place a Basis consultant or two for a limited time, but inevitably the client came back asking for something more (and usually something different), which necessitated sending someone new.

A colleague of mine once claimed to be "grout," meaning he was being asked to fill in all the client cracks. Bringing in consultants to serve as "grout" is a normal response, except that the consultants do not necessarily need to be on-site.

While a local Basis handyman is, well, handy, it may be wiser to outsource most of the following functions, all of which can be done remotely:

- ▶ **Daily monitoring**
  - ▶ Abnormal system activity
  - ▶ Poor system performance
  - ▶ Load distribution across SAP servers
  - ▶ Verification of successful backups

- ▶ Output management
- ▶ Record locking administration
- ▶ Failed update review
- ▶ Notifying users of failed jobs
- ▶ **All database administration (Oracle, SQL Server, DB2, etc.)**
  - ▶ Performing daily monitoring of database health
  - ▶ Checking database logs for abnormal conditions
  - ▶ Monitoring and projecting database growth
  - ▶ Performance and tuning analysis for modifications to the database structure
- ▶ **Operating system administration**
  - ▶ Monitoring of operating system errors
  - ▶ Application of OS patches
  - ▶ OS tuning and proactive maintenance as required by SAP

Wade Walla is the founder of Group:Basis and has provided remote Basis services for several years. When I asked him about the most frequent comment he gets from clients, he replied, "Relief. They are relieved that they no longer have to carry a beeper around 24 hours a day and that they are freed up to do fewer tasks better rather than a multitude of tasks at less-than-optimum levels."

Another advantage of outsourcing Basis support is being able to move your organization out of its own technical echo chamber. As Wade puts it, "If you remain fully internal with one SAP experience and one hardware partner, you will clearly be missing out on the continuous wave of new knowledge, new best practices, and the like."

For example, when you install SAP, it defaults to a particular format in the installer. If you install the development, QAS, and production instances identically (which less-experienced Basis folks will do), you have missed out on a free and easy disaster recovery strategy.

To get out of the "not invented here" (or "we do it all ourselves") mentality, you can engage a company that specializes all the time in all aspects of Basis across an array of clients. An advantage of Basis specialists compared to applications consultants is that Basis work does not require a specific business or industry context. Clearly, an incoming applications consultant needs a ramp-up period to understand a client's business context. Such a ramp-up is much briefer for a Basis specialist.

Further, many companies have operational environments that are fairly stable. That is the point of buying SAP. Why should firms in this condition have to pay full-time salaries to support what is designed to be stable? In other words, why not treat the exceptions as they occur rather than hiring three or four Maytag repairmen?

Another aspect in favor of remote Basis support services is that the Basis workload is much more predictable than the applications support workload. Even more so than the lag-spike chart presented earlier in this chapter, the Basis workload is a series of lag, lag, lag, with periodic and predictable spikes. Support packages come around about every three months. You may upgrade every three to four years (and would probably have a need for outside help for this anyway).

But what about the Monday after you've installed a support package? Is Solitaire on tap for your in-house Basis guy?

Even if you don't go down the line with continuous Basis remote support, you will need an at-hand lifeline for key demand spikes, loss of your in-house resource to illness, retirement, or transfer, or if your firm suffers a physical disaster.

While quality and efficacy of enterprise applications consulting and systems integration are incrementally improving, Basis and other SAP technical expertise is growing exponentially. This is especially evident in the consulting and support environment where Basis specialists are required to keep up their skills to maintain a competitive edge.

Even in a stable environment, motivating in-house Basis support staff is a challenge. The frustrating nature of Basis maintenance is a chronic difficulty that clients have in retaining in-house Basis administrators.

4.8.2 The Cost of Remote Basis Support

Mark Dendinger finds that many clients in small- and medium-sized firms (i.e., less than $750 million in revenues) either do not know that such services are available or are surprised by how economically viable they can be. "Most clients jump at this offering once they understand the affordability and flexibility."

In a stable SAP environment, Basis work is extremely routine, and retaining Basis help is not always easy or even economical. Remote Basis support for the tasks previously listed will cost from $20 to $30 per month per user. Thus, if you have 500 users, your monthly cost will be between $10,000 and $15,000. Other cost variables include the make-up of your applications portfolio (perhaps including non-SAP applications), the version being maintained, and the nature of the user population (such as whether there is a high number of mobile users).

4.9 Conclusion

The first automobiles provided by Ford Motors did not have a passenger seat. However, there was a space next to the driver's seat that contained a toolbox. This was because in those days drivers had to do their own repairs. Still doing so today would be ludicrous for the vast majority of us.

However, there are still countless SAP clients relying on their own ingenuity and toolbox to maintain their SAP engine rather than turning it over to professionals. In the next chapter, we teach you how to retire your toolbox and thrive.

Evolving technology requires evolutionary sourcing. In this chapter, we provide guidance for engaging and assigning both internal and external resources.

5   Staffing, Sourcing, and Evolving

I once took a call from a CIO who claimed that she was receiving numerous unsolicited sales pitches for application outsourcing. She said that in every case, the value proposition was "We can save you money and we have superior SAP talent." To the latter, she commented that her firm had installed SAP 10 years before and that she still had most of her in-house staff, who were "as good as any systems integrator can offer."

While I did not take sides with the argument in favor of the application outsourcers, I did pursue the subject of staffing with the CIO, and she admitted to the following problems:

▶ Inability to bridge a key skills gap (Master Data Management and BI are frequently mentioned.)

▶ Sufficient coverage in one area (say, FI) but a shortfall in another (say, MM)

▶ An inability or unwillingness to satisfactorily upgrade internal skills

Nearly all SAP clients have experienced these staffing challenges. This chapter is intended to help you overcome them.

There are three best practices you should follow:

1. Take advantage of the vast SAP ecosystem.

2. Reserve budget for outside sourcing.

3. Move your applications staff from the "hyphenate" level to the business process expert level.

After some reflection based on our discussion, the CIO amended her claim that her in-house staff was "as good as anything a systems integrator could offer." While this reflection changed nothing about her desire not to outsource, she was newly aware of the need to address her staffing and sourcing methods. As do we all.

5.1 The SAP Ecosystem and the Wisdom of Crowds

There are no renaissance people in the world of SAP. We are all, perforce, specialists, which is why in this book I have relied on several other specialists that comprise my particular ecosystem. In similar fashion, SAP clients would be wise to tap what James Surowiecki dubbed "the wisdom of crowds," for which his central premise is that the combined opinion of an informed group of people will usually be superior to that of a single "expert." Whenever I peruse a list of upcoming SAPPHIRE sessions that relate to subjects in this book, I expect that I will only have the time to attend four or five, and I anticipate expanding my knowledge of SAP as well as expanding my "crowd."

As Joshua Greenbaum puts it, "An ecosystem strategy by definition says that there's more than just one vendor that can deliver the solutions a company needs to stay ahead of its competitors. The 'one vendor, one code base' solution is more and more about delivering a level playing field than a specific strategic advantage. The ecosystems approach in applications—much like the original ecosystem that Mother Nature owns and runs—is based on a 'sum of the parts' message that actually requires synergy in order to succeed."

Joshua also cautions us to "be sure to mark the difference between a real ecosystem and a mere ego-system. The latter, as the name implies, exists largely to make things better for the company at the top. The former, the one that SAP is trying to build, is predicated on mutual benefits for all."

The term "ecosystem" can be easily abused. If you have 50 Twitter followers, for example, you do not have an ecosystem. However, if you have more than 9,000 companies participating in various partner networks globally, 1.4 million individuals participating in your online communities with roughly 25,000 new participants signing up each month and contributing about 6,000 online posts per day, with more than a thousand bloggers commenting on community topics, not to mention more than 300 firms in a consulting partner network, or a thriving user group of 85,000 individuals who work for 1,890 member companies from 17 industries and 90 special interest groups and 38 local chapters, then you have a thriving ecosystem that every SAP client should tap into.

The SAP Community Network (SCN) is comprised of the following:

▶ **Business process expert (BPX) community**
Bridges the gap between business and IT by engaging diverse members in moderated forums, Wikis, and expert blogs to drive process innovation through collaboration, best-practice sharing, and collective learning.

▶ **SAP Developer Network (SDN)**
Enables over 1 million members to co-innovate in a robust, highly collaborative environment using discussion forums, blogs, Wikis, software and tool downloads, e-learning, and specially designed programs.

▶ **SAP BusinessObjects community**
Connects report designers, developers, and users with resources to transform data for making better business decisions using business intelligence and information management solutions.

Beyond the annual ASUG and SAPPHIRE events, there are hundreds of other formal and informal get-togethers of like-minded clients intermingled with industry analysts, consultants, and thought leaders. You can learn about these through the SAP events page on their website, via *searchSAP.com*, and on the ASUG website.

The bottom line is this: While SAP is hard work, individual clients do not have to work alone. Any planning or strategy should involve deployment of the ecosystem, and your applications staff should be plugged into the BPX and SDN communities on a regular basis.

5.2 Staff for Surprises, Not Just the Predictable

When working with clients in the SAP installed base, I find that a high percentage of them resist the thought of bringing in outside consultants, even on a limited basis. Often this resistance is based on bad memories of the implementation project, but more often it is due to what I can only characterize as a misguided sense of self-sufficiency, like that originally expressed by the CIO I mentioned at the beginning of this chapter.

At the same time, most clients invest 100% of their budgets to full-time in-house staff, which impairs the required flexibility to address two of the aforementioned staffing/resource problems:

► Inability to bridge a key skills gap

► Sufficient coverage in one area but a shortfall in another

Resource allocation for SAP support is two parts science and one part guesswork. Therefore, one good strategy is to reserve a percentage of your budget for outside help on the premise that you can't possibly know with full precision exactly what resources you'll need in the future.

For example, if you have a budget of $1 million for support resources, you might have six full-time staff costing $700,000 and a support contract for $300,000 that provides you 3,000 hours (75 weeks) that you can tap as needed. But what about spike requirements for reporting? Basis questions that your staff can't address? Surprise projects? Bridging a skills gap?

Open-ended sourcing across the spectrum from FI-CO to SD, MM, PP, QM, Basis, or even project management will provide you with flexibility and continuity while ensuring that you are not over-staffed in a given discipline.

5.3 Be Your Own Systems Integration Partner

While it would be a stretch to say that we now have a glut of SAP consultants, the fact is there are literally thousands of independents with eight or more years of experience who are aligned with various SAP placement agencies. These are consultants who tired of laboring year-round for firms like Accenture, IBM, Deloitte, and CSC and have gone independent. Many will work through a year-long project and then take three months off. Others find part-time project work to reduce travel. Of course, in many cases, the balance of configuration work can be done remotely.

The classic approach is to short-list three or more firms, send out the request for proposal, assess responses, pick one, and hope you were right. I suggest the following alternative:

Engage your own project manager, preferably from among your already SAP-savvy in-house staff. All other project roles, while vital, pale in comparison in terms of importance. Establish a viable project steering committee that will be charged with aggressive issues resolution.

Then staff your project through outside SAP staffing firms with staunch screening and due diligence. You know that most systems integrators, especially the large ones, will be staffing from their bench. Because of this, you might not be getting SAP consultants with the necessary and precise industry background and

SAP expertise you require. The pool of independent consultants is far deeper than any of the systems integrators' benches, and these independents will cost about 25% to 30% less on an hourly basis. Of course, you will not be wined and dined throughout the selection process, and building your own team will take more time than sitting through PowerPoint-heavy presentations from vendors who wish "to partner with you."

Admittedly, a team comprised in this fashion can lead to some disparity of project approach, since the consultants will come from varying backgrounds and will probably have never worked together before. One key unifier, however, is the ASAP methodology, which *every* SAP consultant on the planet knows quite well.

One potential risk of such an arrangement is that you have little leverage over "the team." If your Deloitte team is performing poorly, you can ring up the partner and blister his ears. Further, independent consultants can usually walk if they so desire. To reduce this risk, we recommend that you offer a project completion bonus. Such a bonus will not only improve consultant retention, but it will be a spur to complete a project on time.

In addition to the skill sets your "smart-sourced" or "crowd-sourced" team will bring, each member can also provide an outsider point of view that will stimulate your staff and expand your SAP knowledge.

According to Mark Dendinger, a veteran of SAP consulting, "smart sourcing means that instead of simply reaching out for given SAP skills you should be finding very specific SAP skills combined with industry experience. After a project, you can even go back to the same consultants for spike requirements, which promises a reasonable amount of continuity and a tangible reduction of risk."

5.4 Beyond "Hyphenates": Business Process Experts

When learning the SAP alphabet, clients quickly become familiar with the shorthand for the various modules: FI, CO, SD, MM, PP, et al. From the R/2 days to the present, these same two-letter acronyms have been used as shorthand definitions for project and support staff assigned to the applications. With time, consultants and in-house staff turned into hyphenates; for example, FI (Financials) specialists who also knew CO (Controlling) became FI-CO. In similar fashion, many SD (Sales & Distribution) specialists also became familiar with MM (Materials Management) to become SD-MM.

While such wingspan has for years been commendable, we are now in a mature phase with SAP. These days, that "hyphenate staff " is *so* yester-millennium.

Jon Reed has been advising SAP/ERP consultants since 1994 (*www.jonerp.com*) and is a certified SAP Mentor for BPX. He finds that, more and more, the traditional "module consultant" is required to move past modules and expand into full-blown process consulting.

"In the past, it was sufficient for a consultant to be a hyphenate: FI-CO, SD-MM, MM-PP," he relates. "Consultants, both internal and external, are increasingly required to stretch their knowledge not only in terms of a horizontal business process, but also in regard to related business measurements at the KPI level."

We agree that traditional "hyphenates" still have value, especially if they can combine SAP technical skills with strong consulting bones and the requisite business knowledge. We also agree that an individual with a mastery of the orders-to-cash business process, combined with experience in configuring the modules that support that process, is worth gold.

Jon adds, "Speaking of business process experts (or BPXers, as they are often referred to in an SAP context), it's important to understand that BPX is not just a vision of where the SAP functional skill set is headed. It's a recognition that IT and business are becoming increasingly intertwined, and the best SAP professionals—the ones your company wants to keep on the softball team—are those chameleons who can walk across the aisle with comfort and talk business or 'tech speak' as needed."

BPXers fall into the crucial realm of business process owners and applications configuration, where business results are directly driven. The old business-asks-IT dynamic is obsolete.

As Jon Reed concludes, "The SAP skills world of the future is a techno-functional convergence, where the suits are sometimes geeks and geeks sometimes wear the suits."

If you already have a configuration team of SD-MM-PP specialists, you have the raw material for an orders-to-cash BPX team. With a dose of FI, MM can cover procure-to-pay. To get there, you have both a horizontal challenge and a vertical challenge:

▶ Horizontal: Stretch the SAP skills through training and exposure to SAP Community Network (et al.).

▶ Vertical: Deepen the business skills through increased contact with business process owners/analysts and super users.

As you mature your SAP solution, the emphasis should increasingly be on the business end. In shorthand terms, your applications staff should become a mirror image of your business process ownership, except that it will possess the requisite SAP skills and still have a foot in traditional IT.

The evolution from a "hyphenate" environment to a BPX environment cannot happen overnight or without resistance from applications specialists who are content to master a narrow environment. This evolution will occur with greater efficiency if your firm has at least a functional version of a business-centric Center of Excellence. As you continue to erode the wall between business and IT (or in Figure 5.1, that dotted line), your applications consulting staff will quite naturally move more confidently through the business aspects, supported by both the business process owners and the super users.

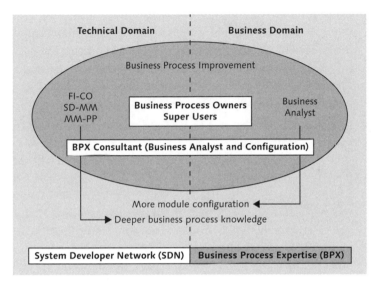

Figure 5.1 BPX—Blurring the Distinction Between Business and IT

Jon Reed provides the following summary of BPX skills:

▶ **Soft skills**

This term is really a cliché; it takes real work to identify the specifics of why soft skills matter. I think of soft skills as the ability to interact as effectively in the company break room as the corporate boardroom. We don't all need to be able to get in front of the dreaded "white board," but we do need to be able to communicate the business case for what we are currently doing. Another misconception about soft skills is that you are stuck with whatever skills you have in that area, but that's not the case. There are many ways to improve soft skills, whether through PowerPoint training, Toastmasters, or even a formal MBA program. It all depends on the specific skills that need improvement.

▶ **Industry know-how**
Increasingly, SAP professionals are expected to bring "industry best practice" knowledge to the table, and this will certainly apply to the BPX skill set of the future. Even technical SAP professionals can add value to their skills by understanding the specifics of their industry, such as by knowing the keys to successful development on retail projects, for example. Knowledge of SAP's own Industry Solution functionality can play a role here as well.

▶ **Knowledge of end-to-end business processes that relate to your SAP skills focus**
While it remains important to have a focused SAP skill set, there is no question that the "big picture" knowledge needed around that skill set continues to grow. Traditionally, many SAP professionals functioned in "silos" such as HR or Financials. Increasingly, SAP customers are approaching SAP ERP in terms of end-to-end business processes such as order-to-cash, procure-to-pay, and the like. Enterprise trends such as information lifecycle management and product lifecycle management also indicate that we need to understand how our skills focus fits into a bigger picture.

▶ **Ability to liaise between the functional and technical teams from the opposite side of the aisle**
It's no accident that the phrase "become a marriage counselor between business and IT," first used on the SAP Community Network by Denis Browne, is often brought up in the context of BPX skills and presentations. The first chapter of this book, SAP Marital Counseling, echoes this sentiment.

Beyond the skills listed here by Jon, your newly minted BPXers should also be moving down the path of business process modeling (BPM). If this seems like back to the future, it is, but this time it is very much in the present.

In past years, clients have extensively used simple tools such as Visio rather than extremely sophisticated tools such as the ARIS toolset. It is understandable that clients would use Visio during an implementation project, since the learning curve for ARIS is quite steep. But I would venture to say that over the long haul after go-live, a client should be prepared to step up to something more sophisticated than Visio. In the end, the important step is to get the BPXers and the business process owners into the same room. After such a momentous accomplishment, I'd be happy if they deployed an Etch A Sketch® as the business process modeler.

Moving your applications staff into BPX mode will do wonders in the never ending quest for business and IT alignment by providing faster results when improving business processes and by bringing SAP that much closer to the business heartbeat.

5.5 The Relative (Un)Importance of Certifications

The certification of individual SAP consultants is a subject of continued evolution and debate. When hiring or engaging an SAP consultant, SAP skills are an obvious requirement; the current SAP certification program does a decent job of testing these skills. It is, however, only a half measure and should take a back seat to a consultant's relative field experience. (In a recent comment string following a blog post about certifications, one person wrote, "I have my own certifications, namely ten completed projects. Do I really need a certificate?" Not in my book.) What this certification does not take into account is business knowledge and consulting skills, which are sometimes known in many quarters as "soft" skills. These "soft skills" should include:

1. The ability to demystify SAP to business people

2. The ability to convince business people why they are better off adopting proven best practices rather than bending the system to meet their personal tastes

3. The ability to write in clear English

4. The ability to work collaboratively with your internal team

5. The ability to effectively provide knowledge transfer to your staff to reduce your dependence on their continued presence.

If you base your hiring decision on a certification process that does not take the above criteria into account, you may end up hiring a drooling and malodorous SAP configuration-savvy maniac that you wouldn't want anywhere near your super users, your children, or your dog. Soft skills, indeed.

For years, I've been pressing for the certification of the systems integrators. SAP dubs its SI partners as platinum, gold, or silver. It bases these designations on number of projects, percentage of SAP-certified consultants and trainers, and—wait for it—levels of SAP product sold. (If you think that's bad, that last one is the only criterion Oracle uses relative to its partner rankings.) If you are engaging a systems integration team, focus more closely on the proposed project manager. We all know that even with a team of highly qualified consultants, a single lousy project manager can drive a project into the ground.

Since certification is focused on SAP technical acumen alone (without business knowledge), I think the certified term should not be "consultant," but rather "SAP engineer."

SAP engineers without business knowledge often build beautiful and efficient bridges to nowhere.

Speaking of bridges, the subject of upgrades is ever in the air. How do you get from here to there? In our next chapter, noted SAP industry analyst Joshua Greenbaum, provides some answers.

Avoiding the uproar around upgrades is not always straightforward. Our guest writer, Joshua Greenbaum, can show you the ropes.

6   The Art of the Upgrade

by Joshua Greenbaum

Upgrades can be painful, and often, the user populace will question stated gains of an upgrade. What follows is a rational roadmap (with checklist) for removing the pain and enhancing the gain.

6.1   The Changing SAP Upgrade Landscape

While all enterprise software customers face the inevitability of upgrading their systems on a periodic basis, many hesitate to follow the upgrade cycles recommended by their vendors. This hesitancy comes from several factors, most of which boil down to an essential, industry-wide truth: Upgrades have historically been complex, time-consuming, and risky, and have often defied attempts at cost justification. And with upgrade failures making headlines with some frequency—anything from complete business shut-downs to costly but eventually resolved delays—this historical perspective isn't without a rational basis.

While upgrade success has improved dramatically, especially in the SAP market, SAP customers continue to be challenged by the complexity, costs, and frequent delays in their upgrade projects; these become even more problematic in a difficult global economy.

The historically high degree of upgrade failure has also helped spawn not only a considerable amount of wisdom about how to avoid disaster, but also a well regarded set of tools and technologies that have been instrumental in turning the tide toward greater success rates and lower overall costs. This is no more the case than in the SAP market, where new best practices and upgrade software have increasingly made upgrade success the norm, not an exception to the rule.

This shifting upgrade landscape makes it imperative that SAP customers take a new look at their upgrade plans and requirements, not just in terms of their ability to guarantee success, but also in terms of making upgrades more comprehensive—and therefore more strategic and cost-effective—than they have been considered in the past.

This is particularly germane when it comes to the relative value of technical and functional upgrades. Many of SAP's customers are in the process of planning or are contemplating a functional upgrade to SAP ECC 6.0—or even SAP Business Suite 7—but with an easier and less risky technical upgrade in mind. The more valuable functional upgrade is on few companies' immediate to-do lists, despite changes in the market that make these upgrades less risky, easier to manage, and less costly than ever before.

It's time to change that mindset. This chapter constitutes a call to action for the SAP community to take a new look at the upgrade process in light of emerging best practices and new technologies. This report offers both the reasoning behind taking this new look—including a discussion of the value of both technical and functional upgrades—as well as a discussion of some of the best practices SAP customers are deploying to enhance the value of their SAP upgrades while lowering overall cost and risk.

6.2   Types of Upgrades

The question of whether to upgrade, or when and how to upgrade, is a matter of constant consternation to SAP managers.

In essence, there are three types of SAP upgrade:

► Technical upgrade, in which the focus is to maintain current functionality

► Functional upgrade, in which system complexity may be reduced and operations streamlined

► Strategic upgrade, in which new and optimized business scenarios are installed as well as a higher version of SAP software

The most common upgrade is a combined technical/functional one in which current functionality is maintained while some aspects of the current system are streamlined or updated.

Many upgrade projects founder due to the classic problem of poor or optimistic planning, which often includes using only in-house staff that may have never accomplished an upgrade.

A wiser course of action is to engage an experienced consulting firm that can bring its experience to bear in ensuring upgrade success. A number of firms offer fixed fee upgrade services that always begin with a brief but essential upgrade questionnaire to address both the current and planned environments. The follow-up to this is an in-depth analysis that addresses key technical aspects:

► Is the proposed upgrade steep (e.g., from version 4.5 to ECC 6.0)?

► Is SAP heavily customized, and what work may be required to upgrade the customizations?

► Is the upgrade accompanied by either the addition of extended applications or a migration/roll-out to other sites?

► Are SAP systems heavily interfaced to other internal business applications?

► Are SAP systems heavily interfaced to external (client, supplier, or bank) applications?

When assessing the need to upgrade, clients tend to identify the following upgrade drivers:

- ▶ **Technical upgrades**
  - ▶ Industry-driven technical innovation
  - ▶ Vendor-driven technical innovation
  - ▶ Business event requirements
  - ▶ Total cost of ownership reduction
  - ▶ Version de-support
  - ▶ Upgrade in preparation for a functional upgrade
- ▶ **Functional upgrades**
  - ▶ Stop or prevent business "pain"
  - ▶ Support new lines of business or business initiatives
  - ▶ Extend/improve existing processes and enhance competitiveness
  - ▶ Satisfy regulatory requirements
  - ▶ Improve efficiency and fill in the white spaces
  - ▶ Initiate or maintain industry best practices

The level to which consulting is required is also largely dependent on a client's internal SAP expertise as well as their past experience.

A firm that has already undergone two or more prior upgrades will be better positioned than a firm that has never upgraded.

As mentioned throughout this book, one often neglected aspect of SAP upgrades is the retraining of end users. I have long observed that the majority of firms tend to spring upgrades on their end-user population and provide little or no training. The result is that end users fail to take advantage of new or extended functionality and, in many cases out of fear, will use fewer of the applications functions than before the upgrade. This also guarantees that business requirements unknown to IT planners will not be part of the upgrade, further short-changing end users who might otherwise have a valid stake in the upgrade's success. It is recommended that firms undergoing functional or strategic applications seek outside help to address these end-user input and training issues.

6.3 Nine Best Practices for Upgrade Success

In virtually every case of implementation failure that I have analyzed over the years, the failure could be traced directly to the people in charge—be they in the internal IT department or employed by an outside systems integrator—and to the processes and best practices they either implemented poorly or failed to implement at all.

This means that the two most important factors in upgrade success are people and process. That in turn means that having the best practices in place can help guide people and process along the road to success. Enterprise Application Consulting's (EAC) analysis of upgrade success and failure in the SAP market has yielded a list of nine best practices that, when adhered to, can help guarantee success (as in help significantly lower the cost and time needed to undertake a technical or functional upgrade).

The following are what I believe are the nine best practices:

1. **Get the stakeholders involved.**
   There is no greater requirement than stakeholder involvement in the success of an upgrade, particularly if that upgrade is to include both a technical and a functional component. In particular, this involvement has to be actively sought by all concerned parties. The IT department or systems integrator that fails to deeply involve line of business (LOB) stakeholders in the upgrade process is courting disaster, because without these users' input the system will likely not be implemented in an optimal fashion. Similarly, the LOB stakeholders who avoid being involved in the upgrade process—even if it is, for the

moment, only a technical upgrade—are guaranteeing that the likelihood that they will actually use the system the way it was implemented will be low at best.

2. **Document everything.**
Every possible aspect of the existing implementation and the upgrade process must be documented to maintain historical continuity throughout the lifecycle of the SAP system. Many upgrade problems are the result of additions or modifications to the system that were poorly or never documented and for which there is no longer any institutional memory regarding how or why the changes were made. This lack of documentation can be a recurring issue throughout the entire lifecycle of the SAP system.

3. **Simulate and test your upgrade.**
One of the best things a company can do to ensure upgrade success is to test the upgrade extensively during the upgrade process, as well as prior to go-live. Many companies accomplish this through the use of a test sandbox, though this approach can add a cumbersome number of iterations to the upgrade process.

Another approach—one that imposes a much lighter burden on IT—is to use a third-party firm to simulate the upgrade and help manage the ongoing testing process. Outside firms that specialize in upgrades are particularly good at streamlining the iterative testing that would be necessary in the sandbox approach, and it virtually eliminates the initial testing phase prior to code changes.

4. **Plan the upgrade well in advance.**
This is a best practice that is often implemented only after a company has had a bad experience with an overly rapid upgrade process. Fundamentally, the longer the time window for managing the upgrade, the lower the risk and the shorter the upgrade switchover will be. This early planning is key to ensuring that upgrade-related interruptions are minimized. As the SAP director at an SAP customer site told EAC, "SAP is our

core system. While we do the actual upgrade, everything stops."

5. **Freeze development well in advance of the upgrade.**
   Another common problem that is relatively easy to avoid is scope creep in the upgrade process. One way this occurs comes from allowing development changes to be implemented as the upgrade is taking place. While it would appear to be a common sense problem that is easy to ignore, the reality is that too many upgrade teams engage in a tug of war with development over what can and cannot be done during the upgrade planning window. While it is possible, with considerable effort, to continue SAP system development during an upgrade process, the result is invariably more complexity and more unexpected problems.

6. **Do a technical upgrade first, but plan for the functional upgrade as well.**
   While there are a number of compelling reasons for the strict separation of technical and functional upgrades in the actual upgrade process, planning for both during the initial planning phase is an extremely helpful activity, regardless of the gap between the completion of the technical upgrade and the start of the functional upgrade. In part, doing this two-part planning can help fulfill the requirement for stakeholder involvement, and it will also help these stakeholders stay in the loop as the technical upgrade groundwork proceeds.

   Having some if not all of the functional upgrade specifications in mind as the technical upgrade unfolds can also help ensure that the upgrade does not run out of steam once the technical phase is done. "In our last upgrade, we neglected to plan follow-on projects" for the functional upgrade, an IT director at an SAP customer told EAC. "We focused so much on the technical upgrade, when we were done with that we just stopped upgrading."

7. **Implement as much standard functionality as possible.**
   This is an old admonition that has historically fallen on deaf

ears in part because SAP R/3 lacked built-in functionality required by some customers and in part because many customers believed that following their own specific business practices was more important than implementing the ones already built into SAP. This prejudice favoring home-grown business practices—especially ones that are non-strategic in terms of efficiency or competitive value—must be reassessed in light of both the extended functionality in ERP 6.0 and the increased cost burden that custom software guarantees, especially during upgrades.

8. **Implement a third-party solution that can help drive the upgrade process.**
   Most successful implementations analyzed by EAC have deployed one of several third-party solutions to assist in managing the upgrade process. Some of these are deployed on-site, while others are deployed in an on-demand manner. Regardless of which third-party solution is selected, the essential issue is ensuring that the upgrade methodology is supported by a strong tool that can provide the necessary level of granularity and upgrade management to accomplish the task.

9. **Implement SAP Solution Manager (though not necessarily before your current upgrade).**
   SAP Solution Manager has several key features that can help not only with implementations and upgrades, but with ongoing maintenance as well. Indeed, SAP Solution Manager is becoming a requirement for companies on SAP Enterprise Support, since it has a number of features that help streamline the support and maintenance of SAP ERP 6.0 and SAP Business Suite 7. EAC believes that companies in the process of an upgrade to SAP ERP 6.0 should complete that upgrade without SAP Solution Manager but then place SAP Solution Manager high on their implementation priority list post-upgrade.

While there is no guarantee that these best practices by themselves will yield a positive upgrade process, the ability of companies to significantly improve on the historical track record of expensive and time-consuming upgrades is well within reach. Combining these best practices with the assistance of an outside firm further helps guarantee success at a significantly lower total cost and with a much more rapid timetable.

In addition to EAC's best practices, Wade Walla of Group:Basis provides these essential technical upgrade tips:

1. **Do Unicode simultaneously.**
   SAP currently requires Unicode on all new installations. You will save yourself an entire testing cycle and oodles of downtime if you just include the Unicode conversion on your upgrade.

2. **Research the SAP website for the latest upgrade tools.**
   SAP has released many, many "one-off" technical "helpers." There are notes, for example, that exist for every module that can point your functional team to the exact areas affected by each upgrade.

3. **Utilize SAP Solution Manager.**
   One exciting item in SAP's latest support package for SAP Solution Manager includes the ability to search and review all custom code and report on modifications.

4. **Don't be afraid to "wave off."**
   Communicate the unknowns to the company beforehand. It's okay to extend your timeframe, because you're performing open-heart surgery here and it's important that you get it right.

5. **Do a hardware refresh simultaneously.**
   This gives you an easy safety valve because you've left the existing infrastructure intact. Also, you'll be able to use the new, super-fast hardware to expedite the upgrade.

6. **Look for an experienced partner.**
   Upgrades are only done every four to six years, thankfully. So don't expect your internal team to do it all. They'll learn plenty, and your project will go much more smoothly.

7. **Demand fixed-bid performance.**
   An experienced partner can easily deliver.

8. **Test all the interfaces.**
   Use the upgrade to force improved documentation of the existing landscape, and test every integration point on the new infrastructure prior to go-live.

9. **Watch out for performance issues.**
   Both prior to and during the upgrade and post-go-live, performance needs to be benchmarked and evaluated. You'll have a major success story to tell the company later.

10. **Expect success.**
    Technical upgrades are one of the most straightforward projects you can do. They have a quick ROI and give you major new capabilities to implement. Go for it!

6.4 Conclusion: The Upgrade as a Competitive Weapon

While the tendency is to view upgrades as a necessary evil in the enterprise software market, the reality is that upgrades can be an important part of a company's overall competitive profile. Ideally, this happens in the case of a functional upgrade, though it can also be the case with a technical upgrade that unleashes a capability (such as Unicode support) that, in turn, opens up new markets and opportunities.

This capability for competitive excellence can be even more readily unleashed when the upgrade process is managed in an efficient and cost-effective way. This process can therefore be part of a strategic plan that can be reliably undertaken without the threat of cost overruns or scheduling problems. Driving upgrades based on accepted best practices is one approach; the addition of bringing in sound outside help to this enlightened view of the upgrade process produces even better results.

EAC believes that lessening the total cost and complexity of all upgrades—both technical and functional—will lower the barriers to the functional upgrades that have been more elusive in the SAP market than is warranted by the potential competitive value they provide. This opening up of the functional upgrade opportunity, particularly in light of the new functionality in SAP ERP 6.0 and SAP Business Suite 7, will provide further leverage to companies' investments in SAP software for many years to come.

To this point in the book, we have concentrated on the how to's of building an efficient and sustainable organization and staffing that organization in a business-centric fashion. Beginning with the next chapter, *Intelligent Business Intelligence*, we will concentrate on ways you can gain continuous and measurable business benefit, which is what having SAP is supposed to be all about.

Intelligence is the key to business success, and SAP's business intelligence is now mature. In this chapter, we provide guidance for using it wisely.

7 Intelligent Business Intelligence

While SAP is a great enabler of horizontal business processes, it should also be the prime source of intelligence for your entire enterprise, from C level to directors to managers and to end users. Many clients have struggled with the implementation of business intelligence or have misunderstood how to deploy their intelligence. Think of such instances as "low intelligence." To assure your level of "high intelligence," I have relied upon input from several enlightened business intelligence consultants, most prominently Mike Garrett and Rob Fiorillo.

7.1 SAP Business Intelligence Matures

The ability to make business decisions based on reliable facts that are presented in an actionable format is the holy grail of responsible business leaders.

Business intelligence is intended to provide this grail. It embraces data mining, query functions, standard reporting (screen or print), and analytics, all of which can be rolled into a dashboard or "business cockpit."

With the 2008 acquisition of the firm Business Objects, SAP moved into a mature business intelligence environment. Prior to this acquisition, clients were generally stuck with SAP's Business Warehouse and BEx Suite and were forced to make do with add-ons such as Cognos (since purchased by IBM) or Crystal Reports (a Business Objects offering).

With SAP BusinessObjects, a client can benefit from a single platform that unites data from SAP and non-SAP sources and allows for the conversion of that data to business intelligence.

With a fully functioning business intelligence solution you can:

► Make more informed business decisions

► Be self-reliant, since you are no longer dependent on programmers to create new reports

► Reduce the burden of data collection and reconciliation in the favor of analysis

As we move beyond the era of IT as an applications factory, differentiation will be based on how an organization manages and measures process change, integrates its service portfolio, and exploits information.

More and more employees are now knowledge workers, and more and better intelligence is needed not only at the management level, but also at the end-user level (especially for customer-facing roles).

We will return to the wonders of BI in a moment, but first, my demurral.

I have to admit up front: The subject of reporting has for years made me cringe. It goes back to my days in industry as an IT manager and CIO when it seemed that I couldn't step out of my office into the hallway without hearing "Where's the listing I asked for?" It felt like I couldn't have a meeting with a business stakeholder without hearing "Without this information, I cannot do my job." Since I entered the world of consulting, these complaints have continued, only with greater variation. "If I don't have this information, trucks won't leave the warehouse." "Without that report, we cannot close a sale." And of course, the doctor who claims that "If I don't have this information at my fingertips right this moment, patients will die."

Often, the arguments in favor of a report or a query are reasonable. However, some years ago, I had a client who was obsessed with getting all the intelligence imaginable. At one point, frustrated with his insistence on obtaining levels of business intelligence that his software could not provide, I told him he would have to be patient "but give me a few years and we'll install telepathic communications." He was taken aback, and I think, for at least a few seconds, he utterly believed me.

Many years earlier, when I was a CIO, our chief commerce officer defined a core sales report that he had to have delivered to his desk every morning, saying it would be impossible to do his job without that information. For a few weeks, I delivered the report myself and laid it perfectly on the corner of his desk.

One day, I forgot to prepare a report but did not receive a call from him seeking it. The next day I purposefully did not deliver it. After about nine working days, I found myself in the CCO's office listening to him describe other reporting requirements. As he did so, his gaze wandered to the corner of his desk. "And I didn't get my core report today," he said.

"Then it's been nine days since you were able to do your job," I replied.

At one end of the spectrum is the executive who craves intelligence for all the right reasons; at the other end of the spectrum is the executive who uses a lack of information as a fig leaf. I've been at this for 36 years and am highly aware that the cravers have too seldom been satisfied. If I had to choose which of these two men I would prefer as a client, it would be the one who believed, if only for a few seconds, that in time he would have telepathic processing. I believe he would know what to do with it, while my former CCO colleague would not.

With SAP, data is more abundant than ever. Much of this data can be information. But information is not intelligence if it is not founded upon business context. Without business context, information serves as fodder by which we can know all the facts of an enterprise but fail to possess the wisdom to turn them into positive action. I make a major argument in the next chapter for KPIs as foundations for positive action, and true business intelligence can take you much further than KPIs.

End of demurral. Thrive on.

7.2   The Data Fur Ball and the Cluttered Toolbox

No firm runs only SAP applications software. Most firms with SAP as their core applications suite have at least a dozen non-SAP applications. Further, we have long observed that even the firms with SAP solutions tend to hang onto unwieldy numbers of legacy systems for no apparent reason. For the applications portfolio-challenged, the result is a hodgepodge of data that is further corrupted by a rat's nest of interfaces. (Parenthetically, I have been running an informal poll over the past five years: Have you ever known a programmer who loves maintaining interfaces? To date, the response is zero.) Data mining tools are keen but only partially effective when it comes to providing intelligence, so the first great challenge in gaining intelligent business intelligence is to overcome the data fur ball you might already possess.

When it comes to reporting/intelligence tools, we find that most Global 2000 firms have more than five separate business intelligence tools, none of which is capable of tapping into the entire enterprise database. Everyone's favorite tool is still the spreadsheet. Some years ago, META Group surveyed 300 firms in the Fortune 500 and found that 93% of them finished quarterly and annual financials with spreadsheets. (Another thing for the auditors to ponder.) Some firms use SAPscript, SAP Query, SAP QuickViewer, ABAP, standard SAP reports, a bit of Crystal Xcelsius (now known as SAP BusinessObjects Dashboards), a dash of Cognos, and for some, as one client once confidently informed me, "We've got BAPIs."

In this light, several clients with various existing tools have asked me whether or not they should adopt SAP BusinessObjects. My basic answer is "Of course." My reasoning is that for business intelligence to be effective, a single source of reliable data is a must, and the adoption of a single tool will reduce confusion and shorten an enterprise-wide learning curve.

These are the top four reasons why clients tend to resist a move to business intelligence:

1. We know we need it, but our data isn't in good enough shape.

2. We do everything in Excel and have everything we need.

3. We've been doing it this way for 30 years and it all works.

4. I don't need visualization. The flat numbers work for me.

1 is by the far the most common and can be addressed. The other three reasons are of the "flat earth" variety and can only be addressed by those who first discover fire, the wheel, and the abacus.

7.3 Sources of Truth

Credibility is at the fulcrum of business intelligence failure or success. If you do not trust your data, your business leaders will not trust their intelligence, so we recommend this essential order of business:

1. Gather the core data, either from SAP or non-SAP sources.

2. Integrate the data and ensure its coherency and integrity (see Figure 7.1).

   Without Master Data Management (MDM) the task of integrating non-SAP data may be onerous, but as we will see, much of the heartache is reduced with SAP BusinessObjects tools.

3. Organize the data into a usable format within a business framework (perhaps into business objects).

4. Convert the business objects into "intelligence" via chosen vehicle (reports, analytics, dashboards, etc.).

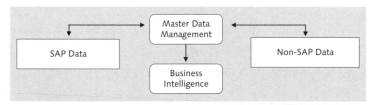

Figure 7.1 Basic Information Architecture

For steps 1, 2, and 3, the most elegant and welcome phrase I hear in connection with SAP BusinessObjects is "sources of truth." This refers to the assignment of a source of data that is the "right" answer to a properly posed query. For example, your firm may have a billing system and a CRM system, both of which contain a client's contact email address. If it is determined that the CRM system is the source of email truth and the billing system email does not match it, then the CRM email will be written back to the billing system.

Such validation and "write back" can also occur during data entry, in which new data can be validated through a source of truth.

Sources of truth are derived first from an SAP BusinessObjects tool known as Data Services, whose first tier is extract, transform, and load (ETL). Data quality is addressed with the Data Integrator, which, among other things, allows you to search for duplicate records and condense them into one, identify the sources of truth for that data, and write it back to other systems. Furthering the cause of credibility is the Metadata Manager, which lets an end user know where the data came from and how it was manipulated to get into the source system via a drill-down of a data item included in business intelligence output. This is known as data lineage, and it contributes mightily to intelligence credibility.

Rob Fiorillo, the founder of RPF Consulting Services and whose insight into business intelligence is much appreciated, describes how his firm helped a client prepare for cutover from a legacy system to SAP: "When the customer needed a purchase order, the data services tool created it with a PO number from SAP that was written back to the source/legacy system. As such, SAP was the source of truth. When it was time to cut over to SAP, all the data was SAP-ready."

Another feature of SAP BusinessObjects that directly serves the vision of a thriving Center of Excellence (as well as step 4 of the previously mentioned order of business) is the application foundation. This incorporates analytic engines with which clients can segment products, track sales revenue, predict customer behavior, and perform similar tasks. These engines include the following:

▶ Metrics for tracking and measuring KPIs over time

▶ Business rules and alerts for automatic notification of change

▶ Sets for segmentation and analysis of business groupings

▶ Predictive analysis for insight into future events

▶ Statistical process controls to support quality control initiatives

While various other means can be used for steps 3 and 4 (Cognos has been a prime option for many SAP clients in the past), SAP BusinessObjects is now central to the SAP product portfolio (see Figure 7.2).

SAP offers a variety of means for expressing the intelligence in its most usable fashion. Crystal Reports has a long history with SAP clientele. I have personally used Xcelsius (in a non-SAP environment) over a number of years, and can testify to its high level of flexibility and clarity of output as well as powerful, visual what-if capabilities.

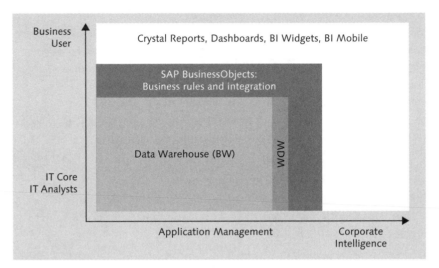

Figure 7.2 The SAP Business Intelligence Portfolio

This shift of intelligence sourcing from IT to business is a welcome evolution, provided that the said LOB user understands the information received and knows how to leverage it in a positive fashion. Which leads to…

7.4 Who Generates What and How and Why?

In the mid-1980s, when I was the equivalent of what is today a CIO, I decided to consider my business stakeholders' constant demand for more information the highest priority. The solution seemed simple enough, as we had recently been able to connect our PCs to the IBM mainframe. Using past reporting requirements as a benchmark, we instituted a daily transfer of key data from the mainframe to various PCs and provided the business stakeholders with query tools by which they could generate the reports they so craved within minutes. This democratic gesture resulted in complete chaos. Sales directors came up with analyses that led them to inadvertently under-price products. Manufacturing foremen rescheduled printing jobs based on shoddy spreadsheets based on the wrong data. Spreadsheet reports clashed with the reports coming from our mainframe.

This colossal mistake had many layers, but the two most damaging were these:

1. The presumption that everyone would understand the nature of information

2. The presumption that information, however unreliable, superseded established process

Another serious weakness of letting business people use spreadsheets for reporting? They can manually change the results to whatever they want them to be. So much for the sources of truth.

The business intelligence tools covered herein do not provide business context. That is your task. And in that light, too many BI projects are done backwards. Consultants often begin with the data and build upward to the upper levels of business management with a "Ta-dah! Here's your intelligence" and a flourish. The problem is that such an approach often leads to intelligence results that are off the mark.

This is a mistake that was long since recognized by Rob Fiorillo, whose firm's methodology is to begin with the highest stakeholders to determine:

1. What intelligence they need

2. How they want the intelligence expressed

3. The hierarchy of end users and analysts

However, as elegantly argued by Mike Garrett in his brilliant *Using Crystal Reports with SAP* (SAP PRESS, 2010), "the classic top-down waterfall methodology assumes that end users know what they want before they get it, or in other words, that they're somehow able to recognize something they've never seen before."

What you must avoid is simply asking a CEO, a vice president, or an end user what information he or she wants. This is especially the case for firms new to the notion of business intelligence, as they tend to be thinking of reports rather than intelligence. Further, the generation of business intelligence must not be a one-time project, but rather an iterative day-to-day (and often just-in-time) process.

With this information, the required data rationalization and consolidation is done in a proper context. Beginning with the leading stakeholders, consultants also have the opportunity to frame expectations and enlighten executives about the best practices for business intelligence deployment. Further, the remainder of the project will be far more driven from the top, since business stakeholders will have already been given a view of the end game.

It is your ongoing duty to constantly frame your business intelligence with context. Without it, your intelligence will simply fuel confusion.

In this light, I would argue that business should *own* the subject, while it could be argued that IT will own the process and business will own the utilization. However, as Mike Garrett argues, "Every transaction recorded in a database had its origin with someone on the business site who initiated, carried out, and completed that transaction ... no business transaction can trace its origin to someone in IT. That's not the job of IT."

Even with business intelligence, clients tend to revert to the "business defines, IT provides" mentality, which, in addition to fatally slowing down the intelligence provision process, keeps business in the dark about that process. And the process is not all that difficult. This is not to say that *all* business people should be generating their own intelligence. It is to say that whatever intelligence is generated has nothing to do with IT. Nothing at all.

Whatever business does with its BI tools, whatever reports they generate, whatever queries they complete, nothing in the IT base is changed. In other words, business can do no harm to a database, a business transaction, or a program. IT-wise, business deployment of business intelligence is risk-free. It is for IT to ensure that the necessary data is "report-ready" and then to get out of the way.

You still have to avoid the problems I created with my PC-to-mainframe connection and recognize that it's hard to find people who both know the business and understand the tools (partly because IT has kept the tools to themselves). Not everyone will qualify, and no, you will not require the CEO to generate his or her own reports. All the same, you should not fool yourselves into thinking that business ownership of its intelligence is an added burden. Simply think of all the meetings you've had in which business defines and IT queries and business re-defines them and IT produces them and business rejects them because, being ignorant of the process, in fact business didn't know how to define its own needs.

The primary purpose of business intelligence will be to drive enterprise strategy and behavior based on a clear reflection of process results and greater business results. There are three dimensions to effective business intelligence: level, view, and purpose. Not all views are required for all levels (see Table 7.1).

Level	View			
	Operational	Historical	Analytical	Predictive
C-Level	X	X	X	X
Director	X	X	X	X
Manager	X	X	X	X
Supervisor	X	X	X	
Super User	X	X		

Table 7.1 Views and Levels of Business Intelligence

View:

- ▶ Operational (what is happening now)
- ▶ Historical (what happened in the past)
- ▶ Analytical (why happenings have occurred)
- ▶ Predictive (what will happen)

Purpose:

- ▶ To learn and improve
- ▶ To report externally and demonstrate compliance
- ▶ To control and monitor people

The intelligence provided at each level should be directly relevant. While super users may vaguely care about the state of the firm's assets, knowing the net present value of assets will not help them fulfill their duties. A freight supervisor will have a keen interest in freight bill accuracy, but that won't be a burning issue for directors or C-level executives.

The tables in Figure 7.3 are thumbprint example hierarchies of KPIs that may guide a client's choice for its own development. They illustrate how different iterations or expressions of similar KPIs relate to various levels in an organization.

In order to track your KPIs, you will need to choose among four key tools are available in the SAP BusinessObjects portfolio:

- ▶ **SAP Crystal Reports**
  Great for ease-of-use, operational reporting, and financial and external reporting. Not so great for what-if or analytical reporting.

- ▶ **SAP BusinessObjects Web Intelligence**
  An end-user content creation tool that is good for ad hoc reporting and data analysis with decent data visualization.

Level	Cost of Sales			
	Operational	Historical	Analytical	Predictive
C-Level	Cost of sales	Rolling cost of sales	Cost of sales trending	Cost of sales forecasting
Director	Divisional cost of sales	Rolling divisional cost of sales	Divisional cost of sales trending	Divisional cost of sales forecasting
Manager	Cost of sales by accounting executive	Rolling cost of sales by accounting executive	Trending cost of sales by accounting executive	Forecast cost of sales by accounting executive
Supervisor	Individual cost of sales	Rolling Individual cost of sales	Trending individual cost of sales	
Super User	Sales order entry correction rate	Rolling sales order entry correction rate		

Level	Financial			
	Operational	Historical	Analytical	Predictive
C-Level	Finance costs as percent of revenues	Rolling finance costs as percent of revenues	Finance costs trending	Finance costs forecasting
Director	Finance FTEs as percent of total FTEs	Rolling finance FTEs as percent of total FTEs	Finance FTE trending	Finance FTE forecasting
Manager	A/R FTEs as percent of FTEs	Rolling A/R FTEs as percent of FTEs	Comparison of FTE level since new software	Forecast of FTE level
Supervisor	A/R transaction error rate	Rolling A/R transaction error rate	Comparison of error rate since new software	
Super User	A/R match discrepancy	Rolling A/R match discrepancy		

Level	Manufacturing			
	Operational	Historical	Analytical	Predictive
C-Level	Production costs as a percent of revenue	Rolling production costs as a percent of revenue	Production costs as a percent of revenue trends	Production costs as a percent of revenue forecast
Director	Production costs as a percent of product line revenue	Rolling production costs as a percent of product line revenue	Trends of production costs as a percent of product line revenue	Forecast of production costs as a percent of product line revenue
Manager	Maintenance costs as percent of production costs	Rolling maintenance costs as percent of production costs	Trends of maintenance costs as percent of production costs	Forecast maintenance costs as percent of production costs
Supervisor	Machine downtime as a percent of total hours	Rolling machine downtime as a percent of total hours	Trends of machine downtime as a percent of total hours	
Super User	Machine downtime causes	Rolling machine downtime causes		

Figure 7.3 KPI Examples

- ▸ **SAP BusinessObjects Analysis (formerly known as Voyager)**
An "Excel pivot table on steroids," in Mike Garrett's esteem. It is not for the casual user and is very strong for data analysis.

- ▸ **SAP BusinessObjects Dashboards (formerly known as Xcelsius)**
A dashboard-based tool with a primary function of what-if analysis and excellent data visualization.

The challenge is to identify, motivate, and train business staff to use these tools and to cultivate a culture in which business intelligence — not individual opinions — drives business decisions.

The potentially positive note about the current state of SAP business intelligence is best summed up by Joshua Greenbaum (*http://ematters.wordpress.com/*):

"The bottom line with business analytics is that they typically appeal to the line-of-business user, and this LOB user is also their primary advocate and buyer. This is a significant departure from both the BI tools and data warehouse side of the market, which have always been more the purview of the IT department, which then parceled out data and reports to the line of business in a now infamous cycle characterized by delays on the part of IT and frustration on the part of the line of business."

Despite my reservations, I now have a growing sense of confidence that firms are moving more in a positive direction in this regard, as we now have increased our ability to gather coherent data into a form that lets us rapidly answer complex business questions, increase our productivity, and decrease our costs with the answers to those questions.

Even so, one key client challenge is a prevalent failure to adequately target and track measurable business benefit. In the next chapter, SAP as the Engine Behind Measurable Business Benefit, we provide a framework for doing just that.

Failure to apply business measures is the most common weakness across the SAP installed base. This chapter details how it should be done and how it will help you sustain a viable Center of Excellence.

8 SAP as the Engine Behind Measurable Business Benefit

As presented in Chapter 1, SAP Marital Counseling, a majority of SAP clients report a failure to measure business results. This failure has been borne out through a large number of SAP maturity assessments. If you feel the need to skip a chapter or two of this book, this chapter should not be one of them.

8.1 The Daily Doughnut

This is a tale of two doughnut suppliers. With one, I phone in my order before 10:00 p.m. With the other, I enter my order online any time before 3:00 a.m.

When I phone in my order, a chatty lady from the doughnut company takes my order and enters it into their sales order system. On occasion, she enters items incorrectly. (Oh, well, stuff happens.) My new order is added to others and, at midnight, another lady analyzes the night orders and updates the baking plan accordingly. At 3:00 a.m. when baking begins, someone runs an update to the production schedule that includes my order. At 4:00 a.m. when baking ends, someone else sifts through the delivery slips and writes up a route order for the delivery trucks. My doughnuts are delivered at 7:01 a.m., and I am asked to pay cash or write a check for them. I am given a receipt, which I promptly throw away.

When I enter my order online, the bakery system automatically updates the baking schedule, packing, delivery routing, and cash flow. At 4:00 a.m., my doughnuts are baked in pre-planned batches and then are boxed with a pre-printed address label that includes a barcode for delivery routing. My doughnuts are delivered to my door at 7:00 a.m., at which time I acknowledge receipt with a magnetic pen. Payment is made automatically. Outside of delivery, my doughnut transaction has required no human intervention and caused zero lags throughout the process.

These doughnut shops are actually the same bakery. The second scenario is after an SAP-enabled transformation.

While many information technology expenditures must be made for technical reasons, the costs related to enterprise applications should all be tied to measurable value. We have noted that the most successful firms in this regard are those that value and support their business process owner. In most firms, support for these individuals tends to fade after software is implemented; the result is a predictable return to small and incremental improvements as time goes on, thus eroding the return on investment.

8.2 Sitting Tight is Not a Winning Option

During the economic downturn of 2000–2003, the market for information technology services cratered as client firms went into a collective paralysis.

Spending freeze. Zero budget. Cost and headcount reduction. Belt tightening.

So far, this Hooverian response to that downturn has not been mirrored in the SAP consulting market, especially in the installed base. Since the more recent downturn that began in 2008, SAP clients are exhibiting more maturity, including a willingness to move toward instance consolidation, process simplification and refinement, and improved user competency. That is not to say that the catchphrase "You have to spend money to make money" has caught fire, but at least we have trended away from paralysis.

One welcome development in recent years has been the (mostly) retired notion that SAP is simply IT and that IT—like any other utility, like gas or electricity—can be scaled down to save costs.

Many years ago when I was a CIO, my firm's president issued a blanket order to all departments to reduce costs by 10%. Without his knowledge, I went to work with each of the department heads to determine ways our IT department could help them reduce costs. It was the most productive exercise we had undertaken in my time at the company, and the potential net gain was a company-wide cost reduction in excess of 12%. The catch is that this included a 15% increase in the IT budget. This was in 1984, and our president thought as much of IT as he did of plumbing. My budget was cut by 10% and I left the firm to get into consulting.

Increasingly, client management, both on the business and IT sides, holds the common view that SAP is a business enabler that can be deployed to (a) save money and (b) increase revenues. How to do both, especially in the wake of the global financial crisis, is the key subject of this chapter.

Bill Wood, a 15-year SAP consultant and SAP project manager who runs *R3Now.com*, says:

"Many companies are beginning to realize some of the culture transformation promised by ERP. The SAP shops who are realizing the benefits have been live long enough that lower-level management and application support are changing from a reactive transaction support mode to more proactive data analysis. This, in turn, leads to better planning and gives the corporate culture a more strategic orientation. That strategic orientation is leading to value-based spending decisions that are producing real benefits."

The next section describes an activity path that should be followed even when the economic weather is fair. One distinction for these economic conditions, however, is a presumption that you will not be adding significant resources or investments; the economic gains that will be realized will be derived from existing resources, with greater focus on value and less focus on the daily grind.

There are two key steps to follow to weather any fiscal challenge with SAP:

1. Liberate yourself from non-strategic activities.

2. Fulfill strategic activities based on targeted and measurable business benefit.

Even in fairly mature SAP installations, there are countless tasks to be fulfilled on a daily basis that provide little or no value to your enterprise. Many of these tasks are "the things we do because they need doing."

Meridian Consulting is a firm I've been associated with for many years that helps clients drive more value with their SAP system. In doing so, they define four types of tasks (see also Table 8.1):

▶ Customer-service tasks entail physical, vocal, or electronic interface(s) with a customer (that is, someone who "consumes"' or derives value from your output). These tasks begin with words like *respond, serve, reply, delivery,* and *support.*

▶ Value-adding tasks lead up to the customer interface, changing the inputs received so that they demonstrably enhance the quality, utility, or cost competitiveness of the end product or service to the customer. Value-adding tasks begin with words like *transform, enhance, connect,* and *complete.*

▶ Process tasks exist solely to mechanically move a process forward. They are usually devoted to creating and managing "tangibles." While some process tasks are needed, they do not add value. Process tasks begin with words like *compile, enter, move, stack, store,* and *collate.*

Note that some process tasks add value in that their completion is a necessity even when the absolute value is low.

▶ Compensating tasks compensate for something that was not done right the first time. They do not add value and should be eliminated. Compensating tasks begin with words like *fix*, *repair*, *redo*, *inspect*, *check*, and *reconcile*.

Not only do compensating tasks not add value, but worse, they also suck the oxygen from your support staff as well as the user community. "On average, organizations spend no more than 30% of their time on true customer service or value-adding work," says Michael Connor, a Managing Partner at Meridian Consulting. "This holds true in firms with mature ERP platforms, which on its surface is surprising. The problem is twofold: First, too many organizations fail to adequately automate work, which means lots of time spent on low-value 'process' work. And second, the extent to which organizations are willing to devote resources to fixing mistakes is alarming, given the lack of reward for such fixes."

Customer-Service Tasks	Process Tasks
Customer-service tasks entail physical, voice, or electronic interface(s) with a customer (i.e. someone who 'consumes' or derives value from your output). Customer-service tasks begin with words like *respond*, *serve*, *reply*, *delivery*, *support*.	Process tasks exist solely to mechanically move a process forward. They are usually devoted to creating and managing 'tangibles.' While some process tasks are needed, they do not add value. Process tasks begin with words like *compile*, *enter*, *move*, *stack*, *store*, *collate*.
Value-Adding Tasks	**Compensating Tasks**
Value-adding tasks lead up to the customer interface, changing the inputs received so that they demonstrably enhance the quality, utility, or cost competitiveness of the end product or service to the customer. Value-adding tasks begin with words like *transform*, *enhance*, *connect*, *complete*.	Compensating tasks compensate for something not being done right the first time. They do not add value and should be eliminated. Compensating tasks begin with words like *fix*, *repair*, *redo*, *inspect*, *check*, *reconcile*.

Table 8.1 Types of Tasks According to Meridian Consulting

As a simple exercise to root out strategic work from non-strategic work, ask each full-time employee in your support group to estimate what percentage of time they dedicate to each of the four activity categories. The result will not be pleasant. Even firms with a fair measure of SAP maturity find that compensating tasks consume at least 25% of their time. Further, such tasks were almost certainly unbudgeted prior to initial go-live, in that fix, repair, redo, inspect, check, and reconcile tasks are the direct results of inadequate response to implementation issues. Further to this point, you might find that an important number of these tasks are due to a failure to retire applications that were supposed to be made obsolete when SAP went live, or are the result of some short-cut customization or "temporary" work-around. What works around comes around.

Relief from non-strategic tasks may require a "strategic initiative" by which your applications are modified or streamlined.

However, one interesting, if nerve-wracking, test is to simply stop fulfilling those tasks in several well-chosen areas. Like many of the "issues" that arise in the course of an implementation, some the supposed "issues" relative to compensation tasks will simply evaporate.

The measure of strategic work is more easily illuminated if the enablement domain of a Center of Excellence is in place. Compensating tasks are often shared between IT techies (fix, repair) and end users (redo, inspect, check, reconcile). In concert, these two groups can weed out tasks that are not driving a business process or ensuring data integrity.

8.3   Measures of Success

If you haven't measured, for whatever reason, now is the time. I am not referring to the various metrics that are only relevant to SAP deployment, but to business measurements that can be tracked with SAP.

To weather a fiscal crisis and to "thrive after go-live," measurement is an absolute requirement. It doesn't have to be a painful experience!

Here the goal is "more for less," and the means to that goal are centered on your ability to measure and your capacity to act. If you are bogged down in the day-to-day operations, that capacity for action will be limited. If you are not capable of measuring, you will fail.

In the *R3Now.com* online article "Using SAP to Improve Revenue and Profitability," Bill Wood wrote, "Technology works best when the rules, metrics, criteria, and the means to acquire, process, or analyze information which supports revenue and profitability are understood and defined."

Chapter 4, We Do It Themselves: Outsourcing SAP Applications Support, advises you to outsource non-strategic activities to gain the capacity to act. As for the measures, we advise simplicity and clarity instead of complexity.

8.3.1 Getting Past Total Cost of Ownership

The most widely accepted measurement of success for SAP implementations has long been total cost of ownership (TCO). This measurement, favored by SAP software vendors, is rapidly losing relevance due to a combination of (a) the rise of value metrics and (b) the inherent flaw in TCO itself, namely that it is only half of a viable ROI equation.

Further, TCO usually encompasses only the implementation period and the first two years of operations, thus addressing a software implementation with a life span far shorter than the 25 to 30 years of most SAP installations.

Often, simple technical considerations, such as obsolete IT installations, lead to a reactionary move to replace old applications with SAP. In many cases, client management underestimates the effort required to implement enterprise-wide software. During a lengthy implementation process, the temptation is often to "get it over with." In such scenarios, benefits fall to the wayside. This is most often the case when the initial vision was cloudy and goals were vague or, as in thousands of cases in the late 1990s, SAP was implemented in a race against Y2K, when benefits were neglected due to time constraints.

In brief, TCO is a pier and not a bridge.

In this same light, pure financial measures will not suffice. Whether you are looking at net present value (NPV), return on investment (ROI), internal rate of return (IRR), or economic value added (EVA), the result will be (a) open to multiple interpretations and (b) of very little value to the business constituents. Further, results do not provide a diagnostic that addresses what needs to be changed to improve the result. In short, they do not provide enough information about how you are or are not driving value from your SAP investments.

Another red herring associated with some of these measures has been repeatedly cited by clients who refuse to engage consultants in gains-sharing arrangements because they feel that factors other than the work undertaken by consultants may contribute just as much to the ultimate economic benefit as the consulting work does. (A simple example is a change in economic climate in parallel to a measurement period.)

Financial measures do not provide a concrete goal that both business people and IT staff can get their arms around. You cannot use "NPV = $20M or Bust" as your operating slogan.

Finally, such measures do not account whatsoever for intangible benefits. Even though measuring the value of such benefits can be slippery, they do exist.

The bottom line is that while financial measures should be employed, you will need something much closer to the business nervous center than such high-level barometers.

8.3.2　Value of IT Methodologies

There are a variety of proven methodologies for measuring the value of IT. Among them are:

- Total Economic Impact (TEI), a Forrester offering
- Val IT, provided by the IT Governance Institute
- Business Value Index (BVI), developed and used by Intel
- Applied Information Economics (AIE), developed by Douglas Hubbard of Hubbard Decision Research

These are all valid methodologies, but the implementation of any one of them will require a pretty fair level of IT sophistication and organizational discipline. Further, while the deployment of any of these methodologies will provide more tangible measures than financial results will, they are still focused on the "value of IT" rather than visible, measurable business benefit. I mention them here to eliminate them as possible driving methodologies for helping you thrive.

8.4　Getting Business to Take the Wheel

To truly achieve visible, measurable business benefit enabled by SAP, your business people will have to get on board—and not just for the duration of a single project.

You will not inspire your business people with generalities about streamlining operations or achieving economies of scale. What is needed is an understandable and relevant target and someone to champion its attainment. Champions are set up to be business heroes.

In the introduction, I related the story of a CIO who failed to take measurements when implementing SAP but later learned how to get business stakeholders to step up. The key was using business language and key performance indicators, or KPIs. These phrases represent the hour-to-hour concerns of business people and should be at the nexus between business and SAP. And if they become your lingua franca, you will surpass business and IT alignment and enter into business and IT dynamism.

Consider the following possibilities:

- ▶ Cost of sales
- ▶ Gross margin
- ▶ Gross profit
- ▶ Operating profit
- ▶ Return on investment
- ▶ Return on sales
- ▶ Return on total assets
- ▶ Yearly expenditures on R&D as a percent of net sales

Clearly, these are some of the prime areas in which most businesses seek to improve.

As a result, a business case should address:

1. Description of the mission (why it is being undertaken and what is the intended result)

2. Project context and priority

3. An assessment of the potential impact on current business for the duration of the project

4. Critical success factors

5. Anticipated economic benefits and rate of return

6. Anticipated strategic benefits and business impact

Most firms adequately develop the first four elements of a business case, but the latter two points are given bullet-point treatment when in fact solid numbers are needed. The intended amount of your financial return and the timeframe in which it will be realized should be decision drivers during your SAP project planning. Thus, you will be able to plan to benefit, rather than tailoring your plan to time and cost alone. By planning to benefit, you are directly addressing your business stakeholder with this idea: We will make you a hero.

8.5 The Enterprise Applications Value Chain

For any enterprise, business results are directly reflected in a profit and loss statement. KPIs that most directly affect P&L results should be identified, as well as the business processes that drive them.

In this value chain (see Figure 8.1), competent users fulfill business processes with SAP software. These processes can be tracked and improved at the level of KPIs to improve the profit and loss. Note that without KPI tracking, you would not know if, or how much, your enterprise performance has improved.

To maximize measurable gains, we recommend that you take the following steps:

▸ Determine which performance indicators are the most vital to your firm and which will most clearly reveal benefit (or lack thereof).

▸ Accurately measure your current performance in these areas; this can be costly and time-consuming because few firms maintain data that relates to business processes.

▸ Determine the current performance measures in your industry sector (average and best performance).

▸ Measure the differences between your current performance and industry averages and bests.

▸ Establish a target to be achieved at the KPI level.

▸ Identify the business processes that drive KPI results.

▸ Improve those business processes with a combination of SAP applications, changes to the process, and assured end-user competence.

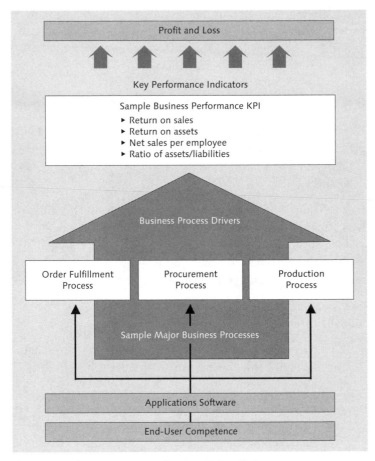

Figure 8.1 The Enterprise Applications Value Chain

End users, who have traditionally been trained only to enterprise applications functions, should be trained for their roles in fulfilling business processes and about how such fulfillment drives business performance improvement. Many firms fail to receive planned benefits simply because the users are not sufficiently competent.

In sum, think of your end users as being the pilots and SAP as the engine as you drive down the superhighway of business processes to improved KPIs that lead to the promised land of improved profit and loss.

8.6 Iterative Business Process Improvement—A Sample Exercise

A prospective client once told me that his firm was in a mess and needed more "computerization." When I attempted to re-frame the discussion toward business improvement with the *help* of computerization, he grew testy, saying, "We're losing five thousand dollars a day and we need to speed things up!" While it may have been wiser to remain silent, I replied that if we merely "sped things up," he could lose ten thousand dollars a day.

I don't know if the firm ever got more computerized. I never set foot in the place again.

While much of what follows reveals how SAP "computerization" can enable business process improvement, the core of the exercise is common sense revealed through measurement. Your business process improvements can be incremental or dramatic, and the decision as to which tactic to adopt will pivot on the required organizational change. Because of organizational complexity, dramatic changes might be more daunting than planned business benefits merit.

In the example in Figure 8.2, the client is a provider of assemble-to-order goods for which speedy order fulfillment is a major KPI. The client has determined that sales order processing is too costly and is a drag on order fulfillment turnaround time.

The client is targeting dramatic reduction in the cost of sales order processing, which, if successful, will yield annual savings of nearly $3 million. Of potentially greater benefit is the goal of shortening the order fulfillment turnaround time (see Figure 8.3).

KPI	Current	Industry Average	Δ	Peer Average	Δ	Target
Cost/Sales Order Processing	$64.00	$52.00	($12.00)	$48.00	($16.00)	$40.00
Business Process	ERP Models			Annual Volume	Annual Cost	Target Gain
Order Fulfillment	Sales, Materials, Management			120,000	$7,680,000	$2,880,000

Figure 8.2 Order Fulfillment Costs

KPI	Current	Industry Average	Δ	Peer Average	Target
Order Fulfillment Turnaround	9.14	8	-1.14	NA	7

Figure 8.3 Order Fulfillment Turnaround Time

It is not necessary to hit these targets in one concerted project. With limited resources, you can effect iterative improvements, each aimed at the same ultimate KPI target.

Measurement begins with the as-is state for the business process (see Figure 8.4).

It consists of measuring the human time required for each step in the process, as well as the lag time (in days) between steps. If your process is more time-intensive, lag can be measured in smaller increments. It is usually sufficient to apply a single average labor cost (resource plus overheads) across a process, as in this example. Note that the $400-per-day labor cost includes the average cost of all steps except for production itself. Thus, 10,000 orders per month are being fulfilled in 1.33 hours (16% of an eight-hour working day), with just in excess of nine working days to complete the process.

As Is									
Sub-Process		**Task**	**Time**	**Step**			**Cumulative**		
				Lag	**Lag %**	**Cost**	**Time**	**Lag**	**Cost**
Sales Order Process	1	Price, Conditions							
	2	Accept/Enter Sales Order							
	3	Order Acknowledgement	0.040	0.040	0.4%	$16.00	0.040	0.040	$16.00
Purchasing	4	Select Vendor	0.010	NA		$4.00			$20.00
	5	Approve Purchase	0.005	NA		$2.00			$22.00
	6	Prepare Purchase Order	0.010	0.500	5.5%	$4.00	0.050	0.540	$26.00
	7	Received/Stock Materials	0.030	5.000	54.7%	$12.00	0.080	5.540	$38.00
Production	8	Plan Production	0.020	0.200	2.2%	$8.00	0.100	5.740	$46.00
	9	Production		1.000	10.9%	$0.00	0.100	6.740	$46.00
Shipping/ Invoicing	10	Packing	0.015	0.300	3.3%	$6.00	0.115	7.040	$52.00
	11	Shipping	0.020	0.100	1.1%	$8.00	0.135	7.140	$60.00
	12	Invoicing	0.010	2.000	21.9%	$4.00	0.145	9.140	$64.00
Labor = $400 per day			Time	Lag					
Total Time and Lag			0.160	9.140		$64.00 Cost per order			
Number of Orders per Month			10,000			$640,000 Cost per month			
Total Workload (Time * Orders)			1,600 Hours per month						

Figure 8.4 As-Is State for Order Fulfillment Process

This business process is deemed important by a client with the following business activity:

Current state/as is:

▶ 500 clients, with 65% of all revenues coming from 60 clients

▶ 500 suppliers with materials purchasing = 60% of all costs

The various steps in the horizontal process are carried out by diverse vertical department—one of the reasons business process ownership is a key issues (see Table 8.2).

Task	Department	Module
Phone Order	Pre-sales	Sales/Distribution
Stock/Delivery Verification		
Accept/Enter order	Sales Order/ Processing	Sales/Distribution
Order Acknowledgement		
Select Vendor	Purchasing	Materials Management
Approve Purchase		
Purchase Materials		
Receive Materials	Warehouse	Materials Management
Production	Production/ Planning	Production
Packing	Warehouse	Materials Management
Shipping		
Invoicing and Collection	Accounting	Financials/Sales/ Distribution

Table 8.2 Process Steps and Departments Responsible

In traditional (non-SAP) arenas, each of these departments may have its own separate IT system, so interfaces are required to pass orders data from one system (and department) to the next. Flow is compromised, as is accountability.

To reach our goals of reducing costs from $64 per order to $40 per order and order fulfillment turnaround from nine-plus days to seven days, we will go through three steps (although, as will be seen, these could all be accomplished in one go). Many firms founder by trying to do too much too soon, resulting in change management issues or too steep a learning curve. In this example we are going to up the stakes with each step.

The first step is a common sense procedural change for which no particular information technology is required. (Most clients have loads of these.) In this example, the client has continued to assign invoicing to accounting, which accounts for the lag between shipping and invoicing. By simply producing invoices at the shipping site, this two-day lag is eliminated and the cost-per-order process is slightly shaved (see Figure 8.5).

To Be (A) Common Sense Procedural Change								
Sub-Process	Task	Time	Step			Cumulative		
			Lag	Lag %	Cost	Time	Lag	Cost
Sales Order Process	1	Price, Conditions						
	2	Accept/Enter Sales Order						
	3	Order Acknowledgement	0.040	0.040	0.6%	$16.00	0.040	0.040	$16.00
Purchasing	4	Select Vendor	0.010	NA		$4.00			$20.00
	5	Approve Purchase	0.005	NA		$2.00			$22.00
	6	Prepare Purchase Order	0.010	0.500	7.0%	$4.00	0.050	0.540	$26.00
	7	Received/Stock Materials	0.030	5.000	70.0%	$12.00	0.080	5.540	$38.00
Production	8	Plan Production	0.020	0.200	2.8%	$8.00	0.100	5.740	$46.00
	9	Production		1.000	14.0%	$0.00	0.100	6.740	$46.00
Shipping/ Invoicing	10	Packing	0.015	0.300	4.2%	$6.00	0.115	7.040	$52.00
	11	Shipping/Invoicing	0.020	0.100	1.4%	$8.00	0.135	7.140	$60.00
	12					$0.00	0.135	7.140	$60.00

	Time	Lag	
Labor = $400 per day	Time	Lag	
Total Time and Lag	0.150	7.140	$60.00 Cost per order
Number of Orders per Month	10,000		$600,000 Cost per month
Total Workload (Time * Orders)	1,500 Hours per month		

Time Reduction	-0.01 per order		$(4.00) Reduced cost per order
Total Time Reduction	-100 Days per month		$(40,000) Reduced cost per month

Figure 8.5   To-Be Common Sense Procedural Change

In a second step, which is technology-driven, we take advantage of web-based order entry, by which clients no longer call in orders but enter them on the web and assign staff to monitor traffic and occasionally help clients through the process. (While the result would be a major reduction in sales order processing, we assume complete adoption of web order entry to simplify this example.) Figure 8.6 shows the to-be matrix.

To Be (B) Technology-Based Procedural Change								
Sub-Process	Task		Time	Step			Cumulative		
				Lag	Lag %	Cost	Time	Lag	Cost
Sales Order Process	1	Monitor Orders							
	2	Assist Clients							
	3	Order Acknowledgement	0.010		0.0%	$4.00	0.010	0.000	$4.00
Purchasing	4	Select Vendor	0.010	NA		$4.00			$8.00
	5	Approve Purchase	0.005	NA		$2.00			$10.00
	6	Prepare Purchase Order	0.010	0.500	7.0%	$4.00	0.020	0.500	$14.00
	7	Received/Stock Materials	0.030	5.000	70.4%	$12.00	0.050	5.500	$26.00
Production	8	Plan Production	0.020	0.200	2.8%	$8.00	0.070	5.700	$34.00
	9	Production		1.000	14.1%	$0.00	0.070	6.700	$34.00
Shipping/ Invoicing	10	Packing	0.015	0.300	4.2%	$6.00	0.085	7.000	$40.00
	11	Shipping/Invoicing	0.020	0.100	1.4%	$8.00	0.105	7.100	$48.00
	12					$0.00	0.105	7.100	$48.00

	Time	Lag	
Labor = $400 per day	Time	Lag	
Total Time and Lag	0.120	7.100	$48.00 Cost per order
Number of Orders per Month	10,000		$480,000 Cost per month
Total Workload (Time * Orders)	1,200 Hours per month		

Time Reduction	-0.03 per order		$(12.00) Reduced cost per order
Total Time Reduction	-300 Days per month		$(120,000) Reduced cost per month

Figure 8.6   To-Be Technology-Based Procedural Change

The result is fairly minor in terms of reducing lag time (from .04 to .01 days per order), but we have reduced the cost another $12 per order.

The third step is an SAP-based procedural change by which SAP-enabled automated purchase processing is implemented. Hereafter, vendor selection and purchase orders will be automated. For this example, we have retained the approval process, but the net gain is another $8 per order and another half day reduction of lag (see Figure 8.7).

				To Be (C) SAP-Enabled Procedural Change					
Sub-Process		**Task**	**Time**	**Step**			**Cumulative**		
				Lag	**Lag %**	**Cost**	**Time**	**Lag**	**Cost**
Sales Order Process	1	Monitor Orders							
	2	Assist Clients							
	3	Order Acknowledgement	0.010		0.0%	$4.00	0.010	0.000	$4.00
Purchasing	4	Select Vendor		NA		$0.00			$4.00
	5	Approve Purchase	0.005	NA		$2.00			$6.00
	6	Prepare Purchase Order		0.500	0.0%	$0.00	0.010	0.000	$6.00
	7	Received/Stock Materials	0.030	0.200	75.8%	$12.00	0.040	5.000	$18.00
Production	8	Plan Production	0.020	1.000	3.0%	$8.00	0.060	5.200	$26.00
	9	Production		1.000	15.2%	$0.00	0.060	6.200	$26.00
Shipping/ Invoicing	10	Packing	0.015	0.300	4.5%	$6.00	0.075	6.500	$32.00
	11	Shipping/Invoicing	0.020	0.100	1.5%	$8.00	0.095	6.600	$40.00
	12					$0.00	0.095	6.600	$40.00

Labor = $400 per day	Time	Lag	
Total Time and Lag	0.100	6.600	$40.00 Cost per order
Number of Orders per Month	10,000		$400,000 Cost per month
Total Workload (Time * Orders)	1,000 Hours per month		

Time Reduction	-0.02 per order	$(8.00) Reduced cost per order
Total Time Reduction	-200 Days per month	$(80,000) Reduced cost per month

Figure 8.7   To-Be SAP-Enabled Procedural Change

The three improvements have allowed us to achieve the goals initially set in the KPI exercise of reducing costs to $40 per order, as well as reducing the order fulfillment turnaround to less than the goal of seven days (see Figure 8.8).

As for the next iteration of order fulfillment process improvement, note that in our new "As-Is" (To Be C), 90% of the lag is due to the five days spent awaiting delivery of materials and the one day of production.

KPI	Current	Industry Average	Δ	Peer Average	Δ	Target
Cost/Sales Order Processing	$64.00	$52.00	($12.00)	$48.00	($16.00)	$40.00

Business Process	ERP Models			Annual Volume	Annual Cost	Target Gain
Order Fulfillment	Sales, Materials, Management			120,000	$7,680,000	$2,880,000

		To Be			C-As-Is	
	As-Is	A	B	C	Gain	Gain %
Time Per Order	0.16	0.015	0.012	0.10	-0.06	-38%
Total Workload	1,600	1,500	1,200	1,000	-600	
Cost Per Order	$64	$60	$48	$40	-$24	
Total Cost Per Month	$640,000	$600,000	$480,000	$400,000	-$240,000	
Turnaround (working days)	9.14	9.1	7.1	6.6	-2.54	-28%

Annual Savings	$2,880,000 = 12 months x $240,000

Figure 8.8 Results

The logical next step to shortening turnaround time would be to improve the materials acquisition process by measuring the as-is steps in the same way we did for the order fulfillment process.

This is only one example of what could be dozens of measurable benefits derived from business improvement enabled by sound business process design and SAP business applications software.

Though this exercise is simple, the key point is that measurement of KPIs should be at the heart of any such effort, and that targeted gains must be measured against the costs associated with them.

8.7 The Deeper Green: Sustainability

While "green" may connote money, it has come to increasingly connote environmental issues as well. While the greater balance of this book addresses the former, this section addresses the latter. *They are not mutually exclusive.*

For several years, Joshua Greenbaum has had the best access to SAP and Oracle senior leadership of any industry analyst. As he wrote in his blog, "Enterprise Matters," (*http://ematters.word press.com*), "SAP's customers, according to SAP, produce one sixth of the world's carbon emissions ... That means that anything SAP can do to support sustainability, efficiency, and other green concepts could have a profound effect on its customers, and therefore a significant quantity of the world's emissions. And, as one of the main goals of SAP's sustainability initiative is to build software solutions that can lower these emissions, and support more efficient and responsible use of other scarce resources like water, enterprise software companies like SAP can indeed become leaders in these efforts."

In the late 1970s, I worked on a Control Data mainframe for the City of St. Paul, Minnesota. The mainframe was a few miles away, and we had our printouts delivered twice a day. One of my key responsibilities was running demographics data for urban planning with powerful (at the time) software called Statistical Package for the Social Sciences. Once or twice a week, I would receive a request for a new extract and, after entering the parameters, I would receive a 20- to 30-page report.

I was only a novice when it came to the full SPSS package, and one morning I made the mistake of checking one extra box that provided a third dimension to the report. Early that afternoon, the delivery man wheeled in a printout that was five feet high. This 10,000-page report was obviously unusable for anything other than a bonfire, but it was summertime and I was not inclined. The next day I instituted paper recycling for St. Paul's Citywide Data Processing.

Today, such an effort would fall under the heading of "Sustainability." In SAP terminology, sustainability addresses environmental, health, and safety issues. At the risk of getting lost amid a flurry of potential avenues in search of sustainability, I advise that you focus on core potential within the SAP-installed base, namely energy and resource conservation, health and safety, and common sense. Investing in sustainability in these areas is the right thing to do, not only in altruistic terms but also because it will improve the health of your enterprise. It should be a given a high priority.

For the moment, sustainability in the context of SAP is a maturing movement. In March of 2009, SAP announced plans to reduce its greenhouse gas emissions to its year-2000 levels by the year 2020. In support of this and other client-based initiatives, they named Peter Graf, a longtime SAP honcho, as its first sustainability officer. In January of 2010, SAP announced its first-year results: "SAP AG (NYSE: SAP) today announced its preliminary report of Greenhouse Gas (GHG) emissions for 2009. The company's worldwide CO_2 emissions for 2009 totaled 425 kilotons, a 16% decrease from the 505 kiloton level of 2008 and well ahead of its established 2009 target. This equates to a monetary savings of approximately €90 million, influenced by both direct internal programs as well as the 2009 global economic slowdown. The emissions decrease was achieved directly without the application of offsets."

Two KPIs are at play here: CO_2 emissions (a 16% decrease) and Euros (found money). As previously pointed out, SAP clients produce one sixth of all worldwide CO_2 emissions. If all of them followed suit, there would be a worldwide decrease of CO_2 commissions by 2.6%, which is nearly equal to the annual rise in global emissions since 2000.

An SAP prospect recently told me that transportation management at his firm consisted of a ballpoint pen and a notepad. Given that his firm spent $5 million a year on transport, it is obvious that basic transport management would save them money.

(I estimated at least $1.5 million.) In sustainability terms, basic transport management would also have reduced carbon emissions. As KPIs go, we could comfortably settle on miles per ton or simply the cost of truck fuel. Since it is in the chicken industry, the firm has other problems. My prospect could quote the hatch rate, a somewhat crucial KPI for this industry, but he also claimed that safety issues were a great concern, though he did not quote any KPIs in that regard.

You do not need a formal "sustainability project." My advice is to embed sustainability issues into business process redesign (especially where the KPIs, like those just mentioned, practically shout to be addressed). This is not a public relations topic unless you have actually done something. If you settle into the standard compliance and reporting elixir offered up by the former Big 4, you may improve compliance and reporting marks without improving the environment at all. However, if you have vastly reduced waste through recycling, reduced carbon emissions through more efficient transport management or manufacturing, or increased plant safety levels, you will have PR gold as well as my admiration.

8.8 Key Performance Indicators: A Basic List

Staff that is involved in setting KPI goals and tracking them must have a thorough understanding of Key Performance Indicators. For one thing, not all PIs deserve the K, as in Figure 8.9.

An enterprise tracking each of the analytic KPIs will be in a better position to improve the major KPIs via a more detailed understanding of what is affecting their results.

KPI targeting and measuring requires:

▸ **An operand**
   What aspect of a business process is being addressed (for example, stock level)?

▶ **A verb**

What is being done to the operand (for example, reduce)?

▶ **A quantifier**

To what degree is the verb being applied to the operand (for example, 15%)?

▶ **Result**

What will be the tangible result (for example, $1 million)?

Thus: We will *reduce* our *stock level* by *15%*, which will result in savings of *$1 million*.

Business Process	Owner	Major KPIs		
		Performance		
Order Fulfillment	John Doe	Turnaround Time	Procurement	Production
		Analytic		
		Automatic procurement %	% Manual Purchases	Manufacturing reject %
		Client order entry on web %	Supplier Query Rate	Late supplier delivery rate
		Order correction %		% of orders revised

Figure 8.9 Order Fulfillment KPIs

The KPI lists that follow are but a small subset of all that can be used. Readers are advised to seek out KPIs directly relative to their industries.

▶ **Over-all performance indicators**

  ▶ Cost of sales

  ▶ Current ratio

  ▶ Debit ratio

  ▶ Gross margin

  ▶ Gross profit

  ▶ Operating profit

- ► Return on investment
- ► Return on sales
- ► Return on total assets
- ► SG&A as a percent of revenue
- ► Yearly expenditures on R&D as a percent of net sales
► **Planning**
- ► Budget cycle time
- ► Budget line items
- ► Forecast accuracy
► **General accounting**
- ► Cost as a percent of revenues
- ► Number employees to revenues
- ► Manual journal entries per FTE
- ► Number of bank accounts and number of banking relationships
► **Period-end close**
- ► Transaction processing
- ► Transaction error rate
- ► Treasury management costs
► **Procurement**
- ► A/P match discrepancy
- ► Automated equipment vs. batch transactions
- ► Cost per purchase order
- ► Receipt transaction processing time
- ► Dollar approval levels
- ► Dollar value of purchases per purchasing employee
- ► EDI percent of total purchase dollars
- ► EDI transaction percent of dollars

- ► MRO order process cycle time
- ► Number of active suppliers
- ► Number of purchases under long-term contract
- ► Number of requisitions
- ► Number of sources for critical material
- ► Number of suppliers
- ► On-time delivery
- ► Percent of purchases on procurement cards
- ► Percent of purchasing employees per total employment
- ► Percentage of minority- and women-owned suppliers
► **Purchases**
  - ► Purchase order process cycle time
  - ► Record integrity (accuracy levels)
  - ► Sales per purchasing employee
  - ► Vendor delivery performance quality (reject rate)
  - ► Vendor delivery performance quantity
► **Quotations**
  - ► Average performance per salesperson
  - ► Average value of sales order
  - ► Frequency of visits
  - ► Lost order analysis percent by reason code
  - ► Order acceptance rate
  - ► Value of offered quotations per period
► **HR and payroll**
  - ► Cost as percent of revenue
  - ► Cost per T&E
  - ► Number of record changes per employee
  - ► Payroll errors per checks generated

- Payroll transactions per $1 billion revenue
- Processing cycle time
- T&E error rate
- T&E reports per FTE (per year)
- Cost to process payroll checks
- **Treasury and cash management**
  - Cash conversion cycle
  - Cost of treasury management percent of revenue
  - Days sales in inventory
  - FTE number as percent of revenue
  - Idle cash balance percent of revenue
  - Number of banking relationships
  - Working capital as a percent of net sales
- **Accounts payable**
  - Cost per invoice
  - Days payments outstanding
  - Headcount per $500 million revenue
  - Invoices per FTE
  - Number of processed invoices
  - Percent of invoices processed via electronic payments
- **Manufacturing**
  - Average order batch size
  - Capacity lost to customer order changes
  - Capacity utilization per shift per work center
  - Labor costs as a percent of total manufacturing costs
  - Machine downtime as a percent of total hours
  - Maintenance costs as a percent of revenue
  - Material costs as a percent of total manufacturing costs

- ▶ Number of changes to schedule
- ▶ Number of overtime hours
- ▶ Number of rush orders
- ▶ Number of web breaks against roll usage
- ▶ Number of web breaks per cycle
- ▶ Order receipt to shipment cycle time
- ▶ Production costs as a percent of revenue
- ▶ Percent of newsprint waste
- ▶ Schedule attainment
- ▶ Setup time
- ▶ Setup time as percent of order run time
- ▶ Spare parts inventory level in dollars
- ▶ Value of received orders press utilization
- ▶ **Inventory management**
  - ▶ Days' supply by part number
  - ▶ Inventory accuracy
  - ▶ Inventory turns (less newsprint)
  - ▶ On-time delivery of customer-supplied material
  - ▶ Percentage of purchased material
  - ▶ Slow-moving and obsolete percent of net sales
  - ▶ Total dollars of inventory
  - ▶ Total dollars of inventory in-transit
  - ▶ Total dollars of SMO inventory
  - ▶ Velocity
- ▶ **Accounts receivable**
  - ▶ A/R cost as a percent of revenue
  - ▶ Annual transaction per A/R employee
  - ▶ Auto-cash hit rate per invoice

- ► Cash application per FTE
- ► Bad debit percent of revenue
- ► Days receivable outstanding
- ► Processing cost per customer invoice
- ► Processing cost per remittance
- ► Receive beyond 60 days as percent of annual credit sales

► **Fixed assets**
- ► Fixed assets percent of revenue
- ► Actual depreciation vs. planned depreciation

► **Sales**
- ► Average sale per customer
- ► Cost of processing a sales order
- ► Number of complaints per ad
- ► Number of complaints per order
- ► Number of delivery complaints
- ► Number of new customers
- ► Number of partial shipments
- ► Order fill rate by customer-requested date
- ► Percentage of repeat sales orders
- ► Returns as a percent of sales
- ► Total dollars of received orders vs. forecast
- ► Total number of sales orders
- ► Total number of sales orders by product group

► **Sustainability (a very partial list)**
- ► Air quality index
- ► Reduced production of acid-forming emissions—emission of greenhouse gases
- ► Waste per production going to landfills

► Water consumption to revenues

► Efficiency of non-renewable resource recovery and use

► Proportion of energy from fossil and non-fossil fuel sources

► Per employee energy consumption

► Job satisfaction index (high rates of job satisfaction are linked to high levels of productivity and creativity)

We recommend these best practices for choosing and deploying KPIs:

1. Establish corporate KPIs first and then the other KPIs in descending and related order.

2. Identify each KPI according to its type: learning, external reporting or compliance, or people-monitoring.

3. Avoid monitoring KPIs that may be abusive or may be harmful to company morale.

4. Review conflicting KPIs and avoid competing goals (e.g., stock reductions and increased production).

5. Avoid the "University of Us" syndrome. Choose KPIs that are most relevant to business process fulfillment for managers, supervisors, and super users. Choose KPIs most relevant to business performance for directors and C-level executives.

6. Rather than merely asking stakeholders what information they want, be prepared to propose the most relevant KPIs in a "dashboard" fashion. Not all stakeholders are aware of what information they need.

For more details, see Chapter 7, Intelligent Business Intelligence.

8.9   Three-Point Planning

Business benefit will be derived by firms that follow this three-point planning on a continuous basis.

1. Liberate yourselves from work that adds no value to your enterprise.

2. Measure your performance, target tangible improvement, and realize benefits through business process improvements.

3. Embed sustainability in all your efforts.

Thrive after go-live.

In the next chapter, Drivers at Work, you will learn how the best practice of continuously improving business processes that are measured by KPIs should be coupled with the best practice of supporting end users who require sufficient competency to fulfill those business processes.

Failure to support the user population will undermine all
of your other efforts. The net effect is that your ROI will
go out the back door.

9 Drivers at Work: Supporting Your SAP End Users

Traditionally, the penultimate project step before go-live has been end-user training. What clients fail to understand is that the long, long lifecycle of SAP means that one round of end-user training is vastly inadequate.

9.1 Skills Gap—Training Canyon

In 1990, a good friend of mine helped an Australian company go live with SAP R/2. Eight years later, he was called back to the client for new work on SAP R/3. In the course of his project, he spent time with many of the people he'd worked with before, and in the course of a pub conversation, he learned that despite a move from R/2 to R/3 and two subsequent upgrades, the users had received zero refresher training in the interim eight years. The effect, they said, was that through time they felt more and more intimidated (or hemmed in) by the applications software and were using even less functionality than in previous years. This intimidation only increased with each new change in functionality.

His account of this experience was my first exposure to the neglect of end users in a long-term deployment of applications software. Clients presume that, once trained, their end-user population will self perpetuate the knowledge base as if the song remained the same. But with each change to a business process, each upgrade, and each customization, the lyrics change and the user chorus grows ugly.

This is all the more disconcerting because, armed with SAP applications, end users are vastly more empowered than they were with traditional stand-alone applications. With SAP integration, a single cause will have multiple effects. This change increases the volume of user competency or lack thereof.

According to Joshua Greenbaum, "inadequate training is so much the norm that you wonder whether failure is much more prevalent than we seem to think or if chance has simply made abject failure rarer than it should be."

9.2 Neglecting The Real Drivers of Business Process

As Harold Hambrose writes in his excellent book, *Wrench in the System: What's Sabotaging Your Business Software and How You Can Release the Power to Innovate* (John Wiley & Sons, 2009), "Only two major industries, one of which is illegal, refer to their ultimate customers as users. In any context, it's an unattractive word, and its connotation of powerlessness and self-victimization denigrates the people it describes and implies that nothing of value could be learned from their experiences."

How much respect does your firm give to the people who fulfill business functions with SAP software? While I have yet to find a firm where "powerlessness and self-victimization" is in the air, I too often find that end users are given far too little respect or attention.

When I get behind the wheel of my Volkswagen Jetta, I don't think of myself as an end user. Instead, I use the term "driver." When it comes to defining roles, our business terminology has failed us in this regard. While directors, managers, and supervisors tend to believe that they are the drivers of the business processes (orders-to-cash, procure-to-pay, et al.), their roles are actually to direct, manage, and supervise those who *truly* drive the business processes.

They are not behind the wheel: The end user is.

You might think that end users would therefore be nurtured or at least supported, but both primary research and considerable field experience clearly reveal that this is not the case.

An early revelation for me came in the form of a survey of installed base firms; 101 of the 133 surveyed characterized their users as sub-standard or failing (see Figure 9.1).

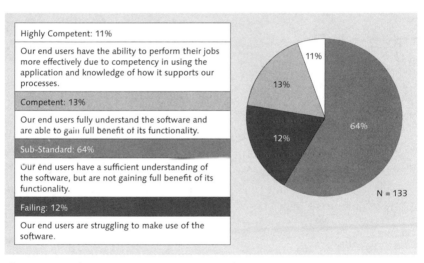

Figure 9.1   End-User Competency Survey Results

Of the firms that were sub-standard and failing, only 6% provided continuous training. In fact, attention to continuous training was a major distinction between companies that have more competent vs. companies that have less competent users (see Figure 9.2).

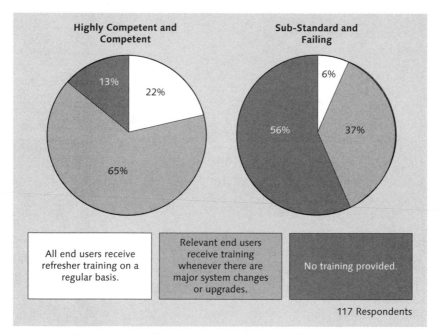

Figure 9.2 Training Activities—Companies with More Competent vs. Companies with Less Competent Users

To put it simply, SAP is the engine that propels your end users to drive on the superhighway of business processes, with the destination of improving KPIs. Expertise is a crucial requirement for your business vehicle; otherwise, it will be constantly in the ditch.

Because users, and only users, directly fulfill business processes, they are the initial key to a value chain of using SAP applications software to navigate business processes while using business intelligence (at the KPI level) as the dashboard to improve your profit and loss.

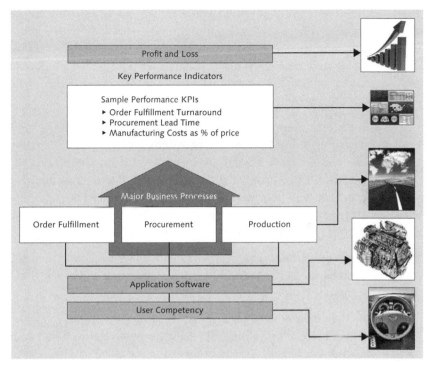

Figure 9.3 Users Are at the Wheel of the Value Superhighway

9.3 The High Cost of Penny Pinching

When economic times are tough, clients tend to make "belt-tightening" adjustments that almost invariably include a reduction of training budgets. Sometimes these cuts make sense ("Do we really need to go to the leadership seminar and golf outing?"), but in the case of SAP end-user competency training, such cuts may cost you more than they save.

Before your firm implemented SAP, you probably changed individual applications (financials, sales order processing, production planning) every three to four years. As such, your end users received new training at every adoption stage of new applications. However, now that you have installed SAP, you are no longer making wholesale application changes and are thus probably not providing refresher training to your SAP end users. At the same time, you almost certainly have no idea that a failure to do so could cost your company big time.

Without some form of continuous support, end users are hopelessly out of sync with changes to the business process, functional upgrades, and transfers or new assignments—all exacerbated by the roughly 10% annual attrition rate. In the latter case, the majority of firms adopt a process in which an outgoing employee trains the replacement, and we have long observed the failure of such a process. ("Perkins! You're fired! Teach Hanson everything you know before clearing out on Friday.")

The result is that user competency degrades over time, and the ensuing inefficiencies and mistakes may make the tough times tougher:

- **Help desk training issues**
  For each help desk call that could be avoided with better end-user competency, at least one hour of productivity is lost. Depending on the nature of the call, business could also suffer (i.e., when the help desk call is related to a sales order entry).

- **Low morale**
  Struggling end users are unhappy, and they will avoid the system as much as possible.

- **Decelerated business process fulfillment**
  See "The Story of Alice" below.

  - Higher levels of transaction errors lead to lost time for corrections, reconciliations, and re-dos.

  - Disconnects exist between end users and business process architects.

  - There is a reduction of cross-functional supports, due to lack of horizontal collaboration, as struggling users are little help to each other.

All of these consequences have price tags that exceed the cost of end-user training. The following story illustrates the most dramatic case of "what could go wrong."

The Story of Alice

Alice (alias) was a senior SAP-trained sales order processing specialist for a firm that considered its users "world class." According to the company's SAP sales order configuration, any order under $10,000 that was directly entered by a salesperson was automatically passed from sales to manufacturing and distribution, thus streamlining the orders-to-cash process. Alice was responsible for reviewing all orders over $10,000.

Since large orders are the life-blood of any firm, it may be presumed that Alice would check these orders the instant they came in. Upon review, however, we found that Alice received no special prompting when a large order was in the queue. To make matters worse, Alice did not check her incoming sales screen on a regular basis. Instead, she waited until the end of the working day to review and approve *the largest orders her company had received that day*. Thus, Alice had fulfilled the business process to the letter while holding up sales orders, adding up to one full day to the orders-to-cash business process. While Alice was trained to the functions of sales order monitoring, she was not aware of her role in the all-important process.

It turned out that the large orders constituted 60% of the company's revenues and that the average delay was half of a work day. Thus 30% of the company business was delayed by a full day due to poor training.

While you might naturally think that Alice should have been aware of this glitch, it must be noted that none of her co-workers, including her immediate supervisor, ever reviewed her role with her. The firm that claimed its user base was "world class" was actually "run of the mill," with a collection of users who knew the features and functions but were clueless about the relative business processes. Should the design have included a prompt when a large order was awaiting review? Perhaps. But no prompt would have been needed if the user knew the business process. The elimination of such "prompt" or "alert" requirements is one excellent example of the virtues of teaching the business process to end users.

But Alice was only one of several end users involved in the process. What if there are delays or errors made in any of the other process steps?

▶ Pricing
▶ Client master record creation or update

> ► Sales order entry or order acknowledgement
> ► Materials purchase request
> ► Purchase approval
> ► Stock receipt
> ► Production planning
> ► Production (itself a major business process)
> ► Packing and shipping
> ► Invoicing
> ► Payment posting
>
> In this basic scenario, up to 11 end users are responsible for effective application deployment. Any one of them could be a second Alice.

In fulfilling continuous end-user training, each step should begin with a review of the business processes before moving on to functions and reporting. All subsequent training will be propelled by this essential context.

New employees without ERP experience tend to compare SAP to outgoing legacy systems and note that they will now have more screens to address, more data to enter, and more transactions to fulfill than before. The first natural instinct may be to resist. This resistance will be largely eliminated if the users understand that they are now using "integrated enterprise software" and that many other tasks related to the legacy organization will now be eliminated.

Business process orientation will necessarily add one half-day to initial end-user training, but users will be primed to avoid the "click here/click there" utilization ruts, and their progress toward the expert plane will be accelerated.

As I make my client rounds, I am no longer shocked (but all the more saddened) to find that senior management has little or no awareness of these concepts. They want to talk to me about Centers of Excellence or business intelligence or extended applications, all while under the illusion that the users are doing just fine.

Here is a snippet of a conversation that I had with a CIO I've known since 1998, and who I consider one of the savviest of SAP leaders in industry:

Me: So how are things going, Bruce? Still thriving after go-live?

Bruce: Clear sailing.

Me: How about your end-user competency? Everyone up to speed?

Bruce: Oh, for sure.

Me: What if I interviewed one or two of them?

Bruce: Uh, hold it. You got me there. I don't really have any idea.

Bruce's company went live in 1999. In the intervening 11 years, there had been no formal user refresher training.

Are you convinced of the importance of your SAP business process drivers (a.k.a end users)? Good. But rectifying a bad situation goes far beyond "more training." To illuminate, what follows are best practices for achieving a high level of competency and maintaining it through the evolution of your applications platform.

9.4 From Inventory to Team Building

At several of my clients, I have found that they can tell me the number of drivers/end users they have by site, but rarely more than that. When I ask about role descriptions or team compositions, I am often met with various versions of blank stares.

To support your end users, your firm must have them inventoried.

Table 9.1 shows a garden-variety set of varying end-user attributes.

User Level	Attributes	Needs
Super driver	An expert who also (a) provides guidance to other end users and/or (b) makes useful recommendations for business process improvements.	A raise
Expert driver	Can fulfill all required tasks as well as crucial troubleshooting. Accelerates the business process.	Recognition
Cruiser	Can fulfill all required tasks and some level of troubleshooting.	Mentoring
Sunday driver	Can fulfill most tasks but does not step beyond known boundaries to learn more (e.g., reporting, exceptions, handling, troubleshooting).	Mentoring and more training
Fair-weather driver	Can fulfill straightforward tasks but requires help for anything "out of the ordinary."	More training (mentoring won't help)
Demolition derby driver	Will hit any key as many times as it takes for whatever function may be imagined and then call the help desk.	An arrest warrant

Table 9.1 Types of End Users

In unsophisticated installations, the majority of end users prove to be Sunday and fair-weather drivers.

A more tangible inventory is obviously in order.

Table 9.2 shows an inventory of two users with the same job function.

Name	Steven Adams	Lauren Beta
Role	Purchase invoice processing	Purchase invoice processing
Direct report	Anderssen	Mikowski
Location	Headquarters	Aberdeen
SAP experience	5 Years	1 Year

Table 9.2 Detailed Documentation on User Competence

Name	Steven Adams	Lauren Beta
Mentor	Alice C.	None
Last training	4 Years	1 Year
Help desk rate	4.6	11.2
Reporting	Daily	None
Reporting	Weekly	
Reporting	Monthly	

Table 9.2 Detailed Documentation on User Competence (Cont.)

If you are keeping help desk statistics by user, such an inventory would be quite helpful in identifying who needs more support, mentoring, or training.

Beyond an individual inventory, end users should be recognized as business process drivers and organized accordingly.

Continuing our use of the orders-to-cash process as an example, Figure 9.4 shows how the team could best be organized and identified.

	Orders to Cash Team					
	Sales Team			**Procurement Team**		
	Pricing	Client Master Maintenance	Sales Order Entry	Materials Purchased Request	Purchase Approval	Stock Receipt
Super User	Evans	Alstrom	Denders	Sampson	Sampson	None
End User	Jones	Beethoven	Blick	Anders	Anderson	Hollis
End User	Smith	Corby	Hollins	Rickson	Singh	LePat
Support		LaGrance			Indio	
	Production Team			**Collection Team**		
	Production Planning	Production	Packing and Shipping	Invoicing	Payment	
Super User	None	Verbal	None	Bermdt	Hollins	
End User	Stevens	Gorman	Jimpson	Brest	Brest	
End User	Barendt	Maxwell				
Support		Lopez			Wang	

Figure 9.4 Team Matrix

When end users are working in teams and sub-teams, they have an improved sense of identity and purpose and a heightened realization of their individual roles in fulfilling business processes. This also paves the way for improved performance monitoring and peer-to-peer mentoring.

Remember: There is not a single end user who is not a driver of at least one business process.

Further, though monitoring and supporting the individual performance of each end user is a worthy activity, there is a more tangible business measurement for this team. The as-is state for the orders-to-cash process shown in Figure 9.5 reaches back to our previous chapter on gaining measurable business improvements.

Sub-Process		Task	Time	Step			Cumulative		
				Lag	Lag %	Cost	Time	Lag	Cost
Sales Order Process	1	Price, Conditions				$0.00			
	2	Accept/Enter Sales Order							
	3	Order Acknowledgement	0.040	0.040	0.4%	$16.00	0.040	0.040	$16.00
Purchasing	4	Select Vendor	0.010	NA		$4.00			$20.00
	5	Approve Purchase	0.005	NA		$2.00			$22.00
	6	Prepare Purchase Order	0.010	0.500	5.5%	$4.00	0.050	0.540	$26.00
	7	Received/Stock Materials	0.030	5.000	54.7%	$12.00	0.080	5.540	$38.00
Production	8	Plan Production	0.020	0.200	2.2%	$8.00	0.100	5.740	$46.00
	9	Production		1.000	10.9%	$0.00	0.100	6.740	$46.00
Shipping/ Invoicing	10	Packing	0.015	0.300	3.3%	$6.00	0.115	7.040	$52.00
	11	Shipping	0.020	0.100	1.1%	$8.00	0.135	7.140	$60.00
	12	Invoicing	0.010	2.000	21.9%	$4.00	0.145	9.140	$64.00

Labor = $400 per day	Time	Lag		
Total Time and Lag	0.160	9.140	$64.00 Cost per order	
Number of Orders per Month	10,000		$640,000 Cost per month	
Total Workload (Time * Orders)	1,600 Hours per month			

Figure 9.5 As-Is State for the Orders-to-Cash Process

Even without such improvements, business processes will be fulfilled more efficiently if the time required by end users to fulfill their tasks can be reduced. Further, the lag between tasks may better be reduced by a cohort of end users who understand their individual roles within the business process. Thus, while iterative process improvements described in that chapter will drive measurable business gains, so will team performance.

9.5 SAP End-User Maturity Model

Table 9.3, like others presented in this book, is derived from the best practices that I have observed since 2001. These practices exceed the simple plane of SAP skills and extend to a more business-oriented dimension.

If you have already implemented SAP, you might presume that you are already at level 4 considerations. This may be the case for the expertise category, but not for ownership/drivers and environment/change management.

It may be onerous to bring in consultants to inventory and rate the skills levels of your individual and collective end-user network. But to gain an understanding of the current state of your end-user competency, I suggest that you complete a self-inventory for each of the best practices included in the model. As for the SAP maturity assessment described in Chapter 2, you should include respondents from a truly representative cross-section of your organization. Ask each respondent to rate your adherence to these practices on a scale of 1 (no way) to 10 (for sure) and assess the collective result.

As previously described, too few firms have established ownership and budget of this subject.

If end users are not included in change management planning, they will be unprepared to adapt to changes resulting from shocks to the application platform.

Whether or not you follow the inventory suggested by the chart in Table 9.3, you should have some means of knowing where you stand, both collectively (across the user population) and individually (for each user).

Level		Ownership/Drivers	Environment/ Change Management	Expertise
1	Planning	Ownership, authority, and budget for end-user training are established within the organization.	End users are prominently included in all change management planning.	Current end-user roles and expertise levels are inventoried.
2	Readiness	Training team, methods, and tools have been established.	End users have received orientation regarding the business goals of SAP adoption and the challenges of an implementation project.	End users have been identified, and new roles and burdens for all are understood.
3	Initial training	The training team has sufficient time, budget, and material.	End users have received basic change management regarding roles, expectations, business process principles, and help desk.	End users have received sufficient training to features, functions, roles within business processes, and ongoing governance/help desk.

Table 9.3 SAP End-User Maturity Model

Level	Ownership/Drivers	Environment/ Change Management	Expertise
4 **Stable operations**	End user competency is being monitored on a regular basis.	Business process changes are communicated to the end-user community, and workplace adjustments are made where needed.	End users are fulfilling key functions within their business processes and help desk trouble tickets relative to training are at a reasonable level (less than 20%).
5 **Expert plane**	A continuous training cycle and budget are established and driven by a recognized entity within the organization.	Portals/interfaces provide users greater visibility and flexibility across applications.	Business process improvements are seamlessly adapted by the end-user base.

Table 9.3 SAP End-User Maturity Model (Cont.)

Level 1: Planning

Your organization needs to fully inventory its end-user population to determine its initial level of understanding and preparedness to move into an SAP environment. In this same light, ownership and budget authority must be established or end-user support will not be sustainable.

Level	Ownership/ Drivers	Environment/ Change Management	Expertise
1 Planning	Ownership, authority, and budget for end-user training are established within the organization.	End users are prominently included in all change management planning.	Current end-user roles and expertise levels are inventoried.

Level 2: Readiness

Orientation regarding the goals of an implementation project must later extend to the changing goals of SAP deployment. The over-riding goal, of course, is the efficient completion of business processes. Beyond this principle, end users should fully understand their roles in your specific business context. How do they contribute? How can they contribute more? What business benefits are derived or lost, depending upon their performance?

Level	Ownership/ Drivers	Environment/ Change Management	Expertise
2 Readiness	Training team, methods, and tools have been established.	End users have received orientation regarding the business goals of SAP adoption and the challenges of an implementation project.	End users have been identified, and new roles and burdens for all are understood.

In similar fashion, the supervisors of users need to be aware of the roles and burdens demanded of end users. My observation is that such awareness usually exists but is not communicated higher up, which leads to an atmosphere in which end users feel neglected.

Level 3: Initial Training

As described in Chapter 3, Building and Sustaining a Center of Excellence, you should have some entity (internal, external, or both) that is driving continuous training.

Mark Dendinger, who was an initial pioneer of the RWD software now known as UPerform, and who has considerable experience pitching continuous training to clients, finds that it is a frustrating endeavor.

"Most of the clients I've encountered over the years have good intentions but no budget or no champion," he said. "Continuous user training is one of those items that never gets high enough on the list of priorities."

Level		Ownership/ Drivers	Environment/ Change Management	Expertise
3	Initial training	The training team has sufficient time, budget, and material.	End users have received basic change management regarding roles, expectations, business process principles, and help desk.	End users have received sufficient training to features, functions, roles within business processes, and ongoing governance/help desk.

End users also need to be aware of what resources are available to them in terms of help desk support, additional training, mentoring, and the like.

Level 4: Stable Operations

This is the maturity level that many firms reach after a year or so of SAP deployment and that leads them to fall asleep at the wheel. Two of these important practices can be met simply by monitoring the level of help desk tickets that relate to training issues. If it is on the rise or already high, you have an obvious diagnostic. Such a solution presumes that you have a professional help desk and sufficient reporting assets to root out training issues.

Level	Ownership/ Drivers	Environment/ Change Management	Expertise
4 Stable operations	End-user competency is being monitored on a regular basis.	Business process changes are communicated to the end user community and workplace adjustments are made where needed.	End users are fulfilling key functions within their business processes and help desk trouble tickets relative to training are at a reasonable level (less than 20%).

Level 5: Expert Plane

One additional aspect of the expert plane that is perhaps beyond the realm of most firms is the measurement of end users in regard to business process fulfillment. This would entail an identification of individual users involved in a given process and a means of monitoring the fulfillment of process steps. One of the burning questions posed to me regularly is this: How do we motivate our end users to improve their competency?

One way would be to institute end-user monitoring in such a fashion and to compensate end users with exceptional performance.

Level		Ownership/ Drivers	Environment/ Change Management	Expertise
5	**Expert plane**	A continuous training cycle and budget are established and driven by a recognized entity within the organization.	Portals/interfaces provide users greater visibility and flexibility across applications.	Business process improvements are seamlessly adapted by the end-user base.

Once you have a handle on the level of competency of each user, you should be able to act appropriately to raise that level incrementally.

9.6 Super Users Provide Super Results

The recognized best practice for maintaining a high level of end-user competency is to have a sustainable super-user network. Super users (also known as power users, subject matter experts, site trainers, etc.) provide inexpensive front-line support to the end user. While the definition of a super user will vary depending upon each organization's charter for their contribution, the following are generally accepted key characteristics:

▶ A super user is an end user who has in-depth knowledge and understanding of SAP system functions and respective business processes utilizing SAP. This individual serves as a "go-to" person within the function to answer specific department-related system functionality and business process questions, and also provides frequent mentoring.

▶ A super user also works closely with the relevant business process owner or sponsor to provide input that will guide business process improvement.

▶ In an ideal environment, the super users are seen as key collaborators to business stakeholders.

In most cases, super users are actual users who dedicate a percentage of their time to support anywhere from 5 to 25 regular users. The percentage of time varies according to each firm's super user job description. In addition to the summary provided above, super users are regularly called upon to do the following:

▶ Troubleshoot systems-related problems and coach colleagues on using them

▶ Train new end users

▶ Assist business process owners in communicating configuration and functionality changes to end users

▶ Continually update their knowledge of the system in their specific area

▶ Participate in super-user meetings or other group activities to share knowledge

▶ Report problems and suggests system and business process enhancements to business process owners

▶ Provide input for ongoing training needs

▶ Help identify and mentor other super users

▶ Participate in user acceptance testing

In my research, assisted by SAP, the estimable Paul Kurchina, and by Julie Stokes of ASUG, I found that the most common impediments to a successful super-user program are:

1. Super users being told by their supervisors to "stick to their *real* jobs"

2. Lack of succession planning

3. Lack of super-user support or respect

The solution to impediment number one is to have a "license" agreement that defines a super-user role that is signed by both the super user and his immediate supervisor. We find that although the use of such a "license" is not contractually binding, it nevertheless tends to be respected in organizations.

The solution to impediment number two is for each super user to identify two nominees capable of replacing them if the need arises.

There are many solutions to impediment number three. The most powerful is active inclusion of the super user in business process improvement activities.

9.7 Sources and Methods of Continuous Training

The firms that provide formal continuous education tend to rely on a single source from super users, the applications support team, and outside sources.

Method	Advantage	Disadvantage
Super user	The user group takes responsibility for making it all work.	Super users do not always know the answer to "why?"
Applications team	Can answer the question "why?"	Not empathetic to user-group concerns.
Outsource	Training specialists are on the scene.	Lack of client context.

Table 9.4 Training Methods

Provided that end users have received business process orientation, the nettlesome question of "why?" should be largely eliminated. Why do I have five screens for that function when I used to have only two? Why do I have to validate this function? Why would I do this before I do that?

In such a case, super users or outside trainers may be the most strategic and cost-effective choice, thus liberating the applications team to focus on improving the business processes.

This leads us to the notion of role-based training as users have become increasingly unique. Back when SAP introduced portals, I spoke with an early adopter who walked me through a functional problem while moving across a variety of applications. At one point I asked, "Are we in SAP now?" His reply: "I never know exactly when I'm in SAP."

In this light, the method or methods deployed are even more important than the source of continuous training, since role-based training cannot be entirely provided to all users. It is now incumbent on users to educate themselves. The following methods exist:

▶ **Mentoring**
This method can best be performed with a super-user approach by which super users mentor individual users. When combined with any of the other training methods, it ensures both personalization and an environment of relevant business context.

▶ **Instructor-led**
An important part of a blended approach, instructor-led training will never be completely replaced by technology because no technology publicly available has been able to replicate the benefits of face-to-face interaction, particularly in the areas of soft skills. My preferred scenario is for super users to regularly provide a "skills uplift" session for small groups of users, and on an annual basis, to have more general sessions led by an outside instructor capable of bringing best practices to your enterprise.

▶ **Computer-based training/CD-ROM**
CD-ROM delivery is convenient, scalable, and bandwidth-friendly. However, this source of training is generic, cannot be related to specific business processes at your firm, and can quickly become outdated. I do not advise inclusion of this method in your mix.

▶ **Online**
There are a variety of online offerings. RWD Technologies offers the most widely used packages. When choosing among the various vendors, selection criteria should include:

  ▶ Simulation capability so the training content will be in your firm's context

  ▶ Tracking/scoring capacity

  ▶ Self-pacing/bookmarking capability

▶ **E-learning delivery platforms**
These are an extension of basic online training offerings that can be categorized into three types according to business application: asynchronous classrooms, synchronous classrooms, and electronic performance support systems (EPSS). Products in this category enable the design, delivery, and tracking of web-based training courses on a small scale and require little IT involvement to install and run. Full-scale e-learning platforms are probably beyond the reach or requirements of firms with fewer than 500 end users.

The worst method of continuous training is having outgoing employees train their replacements. Think about it. Often, one or neither is available for such handover.

There's no doubt about it—training can be boring. Some of the training programs I've seen through the years have interesting features, but the delivery is clumsy, humorless, and stultifying. "If this, then that." "Go back to step 4." "Try again."

What we need is a way to train users by which they will be both motivated and not bored. Toward that end, Joshua Greenbaum and his partners have been working on providing social networking for users and super users as part of an overall "gamification" relative to end-user supports and training. As Joshua puts it: "A gamified Center of Excellence uses game mechanics to solve these issues in business process development and management by enhancing engagement, providing incentives for collaboration and participation, rewarding behaviors that improve outcomes, and generally making the COE significantly more productive and useful.

"By placing all user interactions inside an online community environment, the gamified Center of Excellence is able to support a comprehensive analytics function that can provide real-time feedback and metrics on aspects of community activity, allowing continuous monitoring and improvement of people, knowledge center resources, and business processes."

My experience is that when super users are provided a common communications platform, there are two positive results:

1. Improved collective mentoring skills

2. Improved morale as they feel all the more connected

9.8   Conclusion

A vibrant, competent user population, versed in both SAP functionality and business process, will provide more benefit to your firm than any other aspect of a Center of Excellence. And while morale is difficult to measure, it is obvious that users who are provided guidance and support will have a higher level of job satisfaction than those who are not. The true drivers of this process are your end users. If you are in earnest about driving business value with SAP, you have to invest in those drivers. Continuously.

In terms of improving your overall ecosystem, it should be noted that SAP itself is a constant player in that ecosystem. In the next chapter, we provide guidance for improving the SAP-client relationship as an important factor in "thriving after go-live."

A positive working relationship with SAP will be immensely more fruitful than the traditional vendor-client relationship. Discover the breadth and depth of the SAP ecosystem.

10 From Supplier to Advisor: A New Hat for SAP

The long lifecycle of SAP software makes a client's relationship with SAP a long-term affair. Too many clients allow the relationship to stagnate into a typical vendor-client relationship by which SAP "sells" and the client "resists." However, SAP and its extended ecosystem offer much more than clients presume.

10.1 SAP Life After Functionality

If for no other reason than its substantial (and sunk) cost, very few clients ever switch from SAP to something else. As such, SAP clientele is a captive audience. Before you license SAP software, you are pursued. Once you license, you have been "acquired."

Back in the mid-1990's, that sense of acquisition was absent. Firms installing SAP continued to be courted because of the urgent need for client references and testimonials. (When I started working in the world of SAP in 1995, prospective clients in the U.S. were asking to talk to firms that already had SAP installed. Nearly none could be referenced.)

To improve the client acquisition process, SAP created SAP Consulting in 1997 with the objective of stopping "cheering from the sidelines" and taking a greater direct role in client implementation success.

By 2001, however, the SAP client base had grown quite large. Since then, clients have largely felt captive. For years, they were offered upgrades—most of them related to enhanced functionality—that were presented in fairly magisterial terms and at a pace that was too frequent. The message was "You will upgrade by this date or we will cancel your support."

Since about 2003, when SAP new license sales began to take off again after a four-year lull, there has been a growing sense of neglect among installed base clients. First, there was a great hullabaloo about the revolution of SAP NetWeaver, but for the most part, the clientele shrugged. Since losing the author of SAP NetWeaver, Shai Agassi, in 2006, SAP is talking much less about SAP NetWeaver. At the 2006 North American SAPPHIRE conference, SAP announced an end to upgrades based on increased business functionality. While this announcement did relieve those clients with upgrade fatigue, it also clearly suggests that now SAP can "do it all," which, of course, it cannot without enlightened business-centric organizations.

When firms implement SAP, their business people are given a grand vision of how much more streamlined their processes will be, how much better their reporting, and how in the future the firm will embrace change rather than suffer from it. But after go-live, IT is still in charge, and the tendency is to focus on cost containment, risk avoidance, and consolidations. This is not always due to IT management's desire for such focus; often it is simply the result of corporate dictates.

SAP itself, utterly branded as a technology firm, does far too little to address this misfire. As such, after years of leading its clientele down an acquisition path, it has fallen behind that same clientele when it comes to business-centric software deployment and positioning. The supplier's current preoccupations are SAP HANA (an in-memory computing offering), mobile applications, SAP Business ByDesign (applications for small businesses), and the ever-present SAP NetWeaver. Business is not amused.

10.2 News Flash: SAP is Not a Not-for-Profit

SAP, of course, repeats the mantra about being in partnership with its clients. Whenever any vendor raises this hoary claim, I cannot help but cringe, because the elements of partnership (mutual interest, mutual financial incentives) seldom exist. (Too many systems integrators even go so far as to tell you that they should be your "trusted advisor" even while they are charging you fixed-fee rates.)

While SAP can, in large part, become something of a partner, the foundational fact is that they are a software supplier to whom you paid money for the licenses and continue to pay for support of those licenses. Maintenance revenue is the recurring fee life-blood of any applications software firm, and SAP is no exception. While I often take issue with the amount billed to clients, I am also aware that without the margin they make on maintenance revenue, their profits would be compromised and, by consequence, so would your mutual continuity.

What often infuriates installed base clients is the behavior of the SAP sales force after licensing. Too often, SAP is like a car dealership with a salesman who not only sells you the car, but also sits in the passenger seat and, before you have left the lot, tells you to buy next year's model. Then SAP proper tells you how to drive the car while also nagging you to change the oil, inflate the tires, and speed up before the light changes. Most clients agree that SAP software performs well, is rich in functionality, provides impressive integration features, and can be adapted to changing business environments. These same clients grow annoyed when SAP tells them how to get the most out of the software without paying attention to the clients' specific business contexts.

Right or wrong, some clients do not want to upgrade every third year or so and are quite content to run the version they have in a way they see fit. But in years past, a failure to upgrade according to SAP's timetable has led to threats—or realities—of a lack of version support.

Right or wrong, some clients do not want to retrofit SAP Solution Manager.

Right or wrong, some clients do not want to extend their applications footprint or add a business intelligence layer.

Right or wrong, some clients want to simply shake out their SAP plants and consolidate their gains before moving onward.

Admittedly, with many, many thousands of clients (as well as hundreds of industry and financial analysts and hundreds more technical and services partners), SAP is not lacking in advice. All the same, my recommendation to those in the realm of "partnering" with a captive installed base is to do the following:

1. Buck up your once-impressive levels of R&D.

2. Provide an equitable maintenance arrangement that rewards efficient clients.

3. Stop assuming that you know what's best for the client when it comes to software deployment.

In fairness, SAP has cultivated a rich ecosystem, including the SAP User Group Executive Network (SUGEN), which is comprised of all 31 active user groups around the world, mentoring networks (e.g., the aforementioned BPX program), a new consulting group called Business Transformation Services that focuses on many of the subjects in this book, and a wealth of web-based thought leadership. My complaint is not what they do globally for their collective client base; it is what their sales force often does with individual clients.

10.3 Working Toward Partnership by Leveraging Your Efforts and Investments

Back when the mySAP initiative was launched, there was a lot of confusion among R/3 clients about what it would take to move over to the new platform. SAP's basic policy was that it required new licensing rather than a simple upgrade. What actually occurred was a furious round of negotiation with results falling between these two poles:

▶ **Low end**
Complete re-licensing with no credit for prior years of SAP licensing and maintenance

▶ **High end**
Discounted re-licensing based on credit for prior years of SAP licensing and maintenance

I have worked with clients who have more than 250 instances of SAP and clients who customized the software into oblivion. Such firms tend to take advantage of SAP support resources on a regular basis.

I have also worked with clients who possess a single instance and a single data center, as well as a savvy end-user population. Calls to SAP by such firms are not a burden.

If your firm is a screaming mess, I think you should be paying a high-end maintenance fee. SAP deserves it. But if your consumption of SAP time and intellect is only marginal, you should be paying less.

The negotiations precedent for mySAP should be carried forward into maintenance fees. If you feel your firm is a good SAP citizen and you can back that up with evidence of (a) low- to mid-level consumption of SAP support services and/or (b) internal investments for your own SAP support, then you will have an excellent foundation.

In regard to your consumption of SAP support services, all the stats are already there: number of calls, issues, resolution time, and so on. As far as your internal investments go, there are probably more than you may have considered:

▶ Outsourced help desk (reduces the volume of annoyance calls to SAP through improved routing and service)

- ► High-level or outsourced Basis administration (idem)
- ► Internal Center of Excellence with a strong focus on user competency and robust functionality
- ► High level of participation in ASUG or ASUG-like client-to-client support and sharing of best practices and/or participation in SAP Community Network (SCN)
- ► Full compliance with SAP's upgrade policy (if it is obvious that a 4.7 client is more of a burden than a 6.0 client)

None of this is absolutely measurable, but remember that as an acquired client (and possibly 15 to 20 years of history with SAP), you do not have to simply write a check and sigh. If you are considering licensing more software from SAP, you have even more room for negotiation.

I would also advise that you dial the negotiation to at least one level above your day-to-day SAP sales representative. Their revolving door, especially for small- and mid-market clients, creates a breezeway that does not contribute to fruitful partnership. I know one CIO in the mid-market who no longer even takes a proffered business card when he meets his new SAP account executive. "My Outlook is already littered with names of the departed," he says.

If you are using SAP Consulting for any services, you should have another bargaining chip.

The bottom line is that you should be working with SAP in a partnership mode by which you leverage the efforts you make to reduce the SAP maintenance burden.

10.4 Drive at Your Own Pace (and Show SAP Where You're Going)

I once had a client that continually bought my team's services in increments. First, we completed a small project that improved logistics reporting across multiple sites. Then we fixed some terrible sales order processing software that had been written by a dubious Norwegian firm. We were subsequently asked to extend our services to more of their country offices. After about a year of this, I proposed to the client that we establish an IT strategy to more efficiently advance their evolution. What sunk this boat was my firm's request that we be given foundational insight into the client's company strategy. "We will never share our strategy with outsiders!" they said.

While this response was somewhat draconian, it served as a reminder of the true context of business software; namely, that it is an enabler and business leaders are the enabled.

The fact is that you're not using SAP the way they want you to now, nor will you ever use SAP the way they want you to. Keep the SAP cart behind your business horse. Stick to your strategic guns. Enter your own tired metaphor here.

You can get ahead of the SAP sales curve by involving them in your strategic roadmap. They will pull out their own roadmaps (they have hundreds), but remember that these will divert you into the software subject. Unless your strategy already addresses software, firmly decline and get back to your own plans.

The key is to approach SAP beyond the level of the sales rep. One of SAP's evident strengths is its support ecosystem, which begins at SAP itself and extends to services and technical partners. Where they can increasingly provide help is around your applications architecture (operating system, database, master data management, integration with non-SAP applications, and all other aspects of the big technology tent known as SAP NetWeaver). Other subjects such as value engineering, sustainability, and governance, risk, and compliance (GRC) are currently in the SAP wheelhouse and all merit your attention. Since SAP's acquisition of Business Objects (to insiders, "Bob J."), the organization has committed time, money, and resources into leveraging new business intelligence assets to the benefit of the installed base.

In brief, turning SAP into one of your advisors will not only dampen the sales flame but will also put them into your context where their advice will be more effective.

In our concluding section, I provide some "in-a-nutshell advice" and reveal a bit more about the partners who contributed to this book.

11   Last Word Freak

In the course of a seminar, I was once posed one of those "Can you put it all in a nutshell?" questions. What single piece of advice could I give to a firm that would "wrap it all up in a bow"?

My answer: Be obsessed about business processes.

Everything else described in this book flows from that frame of mind. Business process improvement yields measurable business benefit. SAP assets support continuous business improvement. End users drive business processes with the help of those assets. The effects of business process improvements (or declines) are directly reflected in a P&L statement. Business process enablement and streamlining is the core reason why you have SAP. If it wasn't before you read this book, I trust that it will become so from now on.

12   Postscript: The House I Live In

In early versions of what is now *The New SAP Blue Book: A Concise Business Guide to the World of SAP*, I wrote a chapter entitled "What's Wrong with SAP?" I dropped that chapter after a few updates during reprint because the answers to this question were constantly shifting as SAP evolved. Needless to say, whatever differences I had with SAP in 1998 have all gone by the wayside, including, as I wrote back then, that "SAP is a thin-skinned organization that doesn't take criticism lightly."

In the course of this book, as in many articles and blog posts over the years, I have taken exception to several of SAP's decisions and actions. In the 1990s, I felt that there was way too much unmerited chest-thumping. SAP was indeed making great strides in the marketplace, but the R/3 software at the time was not nearly as functionally mature as was being touted. Later, I was disappointed in a number of SAP initiatives in the small- and mid-sized market and a continual insistence that more software was the answer to any problems their clients faced. More recently, I have become concerned that several SAP initiatives (such as Duet and SAP Business ByDesign) have distracted the company from the necessary path of improving the client experience.

Despite these criticisms, there have been two points in my career in which I chose to work in the fields of SAP. First, after a 10-year run as a "generic" consultant running design build run teams for integrated applications, I felt compelled in 1995 to choose a vendor as generic consulting was being replaced by burgeoning applications software firms. Through the summer of 1995, I looked closely at "the big three": SAP, PeopleSoft, and Oracle. PeopleSoft sounded cool but appeared to be a provider of HR, payroll, and some financials as opposed to being a full-scale ERP firm. Scratch PeopleSoft.

I chose SAP over Oracle for three key reasons:

1. Former colleagues advised that SAP would fit me like a glove.
2. I noted that SAP had a much higher market profile than Oracle.
3. I noted that Oracle was first and foremost a technology firm and consequently, its applications software business was second citizen in the realm.

There followed six years in which I worked as an SAP consultant, concentrating not on how SAP worked but on what it could do for business.

The second time I chose SAP was in 2007 after a six-year stint as an industry analyst, during which time I had considerable contact with all the major software vendors and large systems integrators. Given that exposure, I could have worked under the Oracle umbrella, but I was not at all tempted in that direction. It was bad enough that Oracle had muddied the market waters with an aggressive acquisitions run (J.D. Edwards, PeopleSoft, Siebel, and a host of others) that turned it into a K-Mart of applications. Worse, I had observed what appeared to be an alarming revolving door in Oracle's middle management, a cutthroat sales environment, antagonistic analyst relations, and a company-wide cavalier attitude regarding its clients. All of this was in stark contrast to SAP's relative management stability and apparently sincere attention to its clientele. While they have never taken criticism lightly, they do not shoot the messengers of such criticism. In fact, they engage their critics, myself included, both as a way to defuse the criticism and to listen.

In recent years, analysts and SAP competitors have tried to give the impression that SAP is "so yesterday," as Software as a Service (SaaS), the cloud, and SOA are seen as the pivot points to the future. Infor, which acquired more than 31 separate companies, is now marketing on a theme that "big ERP is over," implying that SAP is going the way of the dinosaurs. Clearly, I disagree with these analysts and with Infor.

I cannot imagine a firm with 5,000 or more active users putting their data out to a cloud. I cannot imagine a firm with 5,000 or more users accepting that they have no way to change their applications software functions.

Nor can I imagine a firm that is already using SAP—and, beyond implementation costs, has already invested millions upon millions of dollars in deployment—to simply shrug and move to something else. In fact, I haven't seen it happen in my many years around SAP.

SAP is the house I live in because the software works and I don't have to know all that much about the technology to help clients move ahead. The functional span of SAP is unparalleled, not only across business functions but across discrete industries. Best business practices are truly best business practices. Upper management is stable, relatively harmonious, and nearly always open to discussion. SAP is no longer the hot new thing it was back in 1995; it is now a mature business with a rich ecosystem and a vast number of satisfied clients from whom I continually learn new best practices. While I will continue to insist upon evolution—my goal is for SAP to become a business solutions firm and not an applications software vendor—I will not be changing residence soon.

Appendices

A   Sources

A book's worth of advice should never be based merely on an author's "experience" and "insight." While it is evident that much of this book is derived from my own background as an SAP consultant and industry analyst, I continue to be educated by a collection of friends, colleagues, and readers of *The New SAP Blue Book*.

Consequently, the contents of this book are largely the result of "collective insight."

While at META Group (now folded into Gartner Inc.) and Performance Monitor from 2001 to mid-2007, I had the pleasure of satisfying much of my curiosity about what does and doesn't work in the realm of SAP/ERP. Over a six-and-half-year period, I led or participated in a variety of studies supported by deep client input, including these topics (at META Group):

Subject	Respondents	Year
ERP installed base	466	2002
The state of ERP services	437	2003
The state of CRM services	355	2002
The state of CRM services	263	2004
Applications management services	315	2003
ERP end-user competency	142	2003

From mid-2005 to mid-2007, working in my own firm, I upped the ante in regard to both data quality (through improved filtering) and quantity.

Subject	Respondents	Year
SAP systems integrators	693	2005
Oracle systems integrators	645	2005
People Soft systems integrators	666	2005
SAP systems integrators	809	2007
Oracle systems integrators	864	2007
CRM systems integrators	709	2006
Application outsourcing firms	709	2006
Application development and maintenance firms	864	2006

While the latter studies were focused on the field performance of service providers, there was a considerable amount of input about goal attainment, issues and resolutions, implementation or deployment best and worst practices, and "data narratives" that described client/respondent priority shifts after go-live.

Among the most striking lessons learned across these studies (in no particular order):

1. **You get what you pay for**
   Fixed-fee implementation projects are the least successful; value-based fee projects are the most successful (if you can measure).

2. **Desperately seeking...**
   The primary reason clients opt to outsource SAP applications support is the desire to obtain hard-to-find SAP skills.

3. **Tell me if you've heard this one before**
   The large systems integrators tend to perform fairly well in the Fortune 500 market and very poorly in all other markets.

4. **Latch-key kids**
   End users can't get their parents' attention.

5. **I said I wanted chicken but now I want steak and later I will be happy to have a hot dog**
The client group mind-set changes radically between the time they choose a systems integrator and the time they start a project. Then nearly everything changes again after go-live. (Moral: It is good to have an articulated long-term vision before starting down the SAP path.)

6. **My last confession was during business blueprint (the privacy of the confessional)**
In public settings, clients blame SAP or their systems integrator for project issues. When provided an anonymous platform for evaluation, they place far more blame on themselves.

7. **A day at the dentist**
Measurement of business performance is deemed (incorrectly) as painful as root canal.

Across the years, clients are making progress, but it is incremental instead of in leaps and bounds. Since 2002, clients have become more SAP self-reliant and less dependent upon systems integrators (after go-live). More clients are adopting a long-term approach to SAP evolution, and fewer clients are mangling their applications with unnecessary customizations.

B   The Author

Michael Doane is an Executive Consultant at CGI. He has more than 35 years of business and information systems experience, including industry, enterprise applications consulting, and as an industry analyst.

In addition to prior roles as an SAP practice lead at Grant Thornton and The Consulting Alliance, Michael has directed several major consulting engagements for large systems integrators, most notably in financials and logistics, in North America, Europe, and Asia. Prior to entering the world of consulting, he was the European IS director for the Plessey Company Ltd. and for Ferry Peter, a division of Wiggins Teape.

He has been publishing information about SAP since 1996. In addition to this book, he is the author of *The New SAP Blue Book: A Concise Business Guide to the World of SAP* and co-author, with Jon Reed, of *The SAP Consultant Handbook*.

C   Contributors

Michael Connor is founder and CEO of Meridian Consulting (*www.meridian-us.com*) and a significant contributor to *The New SAP Blue Book: A Concise Business Guide to the World of SAP*. We have been sharing intelligence and collaborating with clients since 1997.

Jon Reed has been advising clients and consultants for more than 15 years and is now the recognized leader in the field of SAP career guidance. We have been working together in the SAP fields since 1995. His website is *www.jonERP.com*.

Joshua Greenbaum is an independent industry analyst who writes for SAP publications and is a valued advisor to upper management at SAP, Oracle, and other enterprise applications software firms. His website is *http://ematters.wordpress.com/*.

Mark Dendinger has led several successful SAP systems integration firms since 1995, has extensive contacts with SAP America, and has a vast network of SAP consultants.

Kay Tailor is an accomplished SAP architect and technician who has been active in the SAP fields since the mid 1990s.

Wade Walla is the founder of Group:Basis and has a considerable ability to demystify "the technical."

Dane Anderson has worked as an IT outsourcing provider and, since 2003, has been a prominent industry analyst covering the IT services and outsourcing marketplace.

John Ziegler was among the first group of non-European consultants at SAP America. He has managed dozens of SAP projects since 1992.

Bill Wood has spent more than 15 years helping clients go live with SAP. His website is *www.r3now.com*.

Brian Dahill has long been recognized as a pioneer in the evolution of SAP-powered Centers of Excellence.

Index

Gerhard Oswald, Uwe Hommel

SAP Enterprise Support
ASAP to Run SAP

This book provides IT managers and decision makers with a detailed
guide to SAP Enterprise Support. Using a top-down approach, the
book begins by explaining why Enterprise Support was introduced, and
then details the concrete benefits and concepts of Enterprise Support.
It teaches you how and why to use Enterprise Support and covers the
new services that have been included in the portfolio. This is the one
book you need to really understand what SAP Enterprise Support can
do for your organization. This 2nd edition has been updated and significantly extended.

371 pp., 2010, 59,95 Euro / US$ 59.95
ISBN 978-1-59229-349-0
www.sap-press.com

Greg Chase, Rukhshaan Omar, Ann Rosenberg,
Mark von Rosing, James Taylor

Applying Real-World BPM in an SAP Environment

Managing your business processes wisely is key to stay ahead of your competitors! This book is your guide to implementing Business Process Management in all its aspects in your SAP-centric business and IT: It explains how BPM and standard software work together, how to prepare your company for the project, and how to put technology, governance, and the philosophy behind it in action. Extensive use cases from well-known SAP customers including technical and process details make this book a true real-world experience!

698 pp., 2011, 69,95 Euro / US$ 69.95
ISBN 978-1-59229-343-8
www.sap-press.com

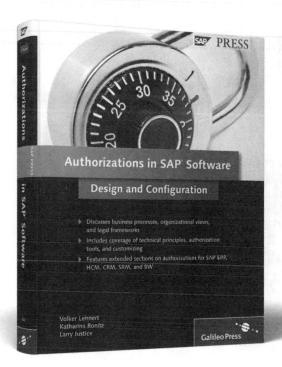

Volker Lehnert, Katharina Bonitz, Larry Justice

Authorizations in SAP Software: Design and Configuration

This book gives you a practical and comprehensive overview of the design and management of authorizations in SAP. You'll learn how to develop a meaningful authorization concept that meets statutory requirements and is tailored to your business processes, as well as how those processes are implemented as authorizations in your SAP system. You'll learn about SAP NetWeaver IdM, CUA, SAP BusinessObjects Access Control, and the UME. Finally, you'll discover how to implement an authorizations concept in various other SAP applications and components (SAP ERP, HCM, CRM, SRM, and BW).

684 pp., 2010, 79,95 Euro / US$ 79.95
ISBN 978-1-59229-342-1
www.sap-press.com

Loren Heilig, Peter Gergen, Andreas Müller

Understanding SAP NetWeaver Identity Management

Whether you're thinking about an identity management solution for your company, are currently implementing one, or are already working with SAP NetWeaver Identity Management, this book covers all important aspects for the selection, implementation, and operation of the solution. Take advantage of proven concepts and tips from the authors, and learn SAP NetWeaver IdM from A to Z.

300 pp., 2010, 69,95 Euro / US$ 69.95
ISBN 978-1-59229-338-4
www.sap-press.com

Olaf Schulz

Using SAP: A Guide for Beginners and End Users

This book helps end users and beginners get started in SAP ERP and provides readers with the basic knowledge they need for their daily work. Readers will get to know the essentials of working with the SAP system, learn about the SAP systems' structures and functions, and discover how SAP connects to critical business processes. Whether this book is used as an exercise book or as a reference book, readers will find what they need to help them become more comfortable with SAP ERP.

388 pp., 2012, 39,95 Euro / US$ 39.95
ISBN 978-1-59229-408-4

www.sap-press.com